William Humphrey

Mary magnifying God: May Sermons

William Humphrey

Mary magnifying God: May Sermons

ISBN/EAN: 9783743349476

Manufactured in Europe, USA, Canada, Australia, Japa

Cover: Foto ©Lupo / pixelio.de

Manufactured and distributed by brebook publishing software (www.brebook.com)

William Humphrey

Mary magnifying God: May Sermons

MARY MAGNIFYING GOD.

May Sermons.

By WILLIAM HUMPHREY,

OF THE CONGREGATION OF THE OBLATES OF ST. CHARLES.

LONDON: BURNS AND OATES,

Portman Street and Paternoster Row.

1873.

Nihil obstat.

FRANCISCUS WYNDHAM,
Ex Cong. Oblat. S. Caroli, Censor Deputatus.

Imprimatur.

✠ HENRICUS EDUARDUS,
Archiepiscopus Westmonast.

In Festo Annuntiationis B.M.V., 1873.

PREFACE.

To readers of St. Ephrem, St. Bernard, St. Alphonsus, and Father Faber, the language of the following Sermons will seem hard and cold. The writer's apology for this is, that they are mainly dogmatic or doctrinal, and not directly devotional. The language of dogma is necessarily measured. Statements of doctrine, moreover, will be substantially the same by whomsoever they are uttered, or to whomsoever they are addressed. With the language of devotion it is otherwise. It differs widely with the differences of individual temperament, circumstances, and attraction. It differs in different ages, in different countries, with men of different races and of different classes. It differs also with the differences of age and sex.

Their dogmatic character, then, will account in great measure for the language of restraint in these Sermons. A reason for this character was the writer's conviction of the necessity—and the

special necessity in our day—of a solid dogmatic
basis as an indispensable foundation for true devotion.   Devotion divorced from dogma becomes
mere pious sentiment.   It is not the service of the
whole man; and it is not the service of man—as
man.   It is not a *rationabile obsequium.*   Thinking
and practical men will turn away from mere pious
prettiness; they may be attracted by theological
beauty.   Those two are by no means convertible
terms.

Finally, the aim of the writer has been to
show that Mary has her place in Christian Theo-
logy as really as she has her place in the economy
of the Incarnation;—that devotion to her is not
an ornamental addition or a beautiful outgrowth
of Christianity, but an essential constituent and
necessary part.   A christianity in which Mary has
not a place, and her own place, is *aliud evangelium,
quod non est aliud*—' another gospel, which is not
another.'

St. Mary of the Angels, Bayswater, London, W.
Lady-day 1873.

CONTENTS.

I.

IT is a wonderful thought, full to us of consolation and of strength, that the highest and noblest and most perfect of creatures, and that creature which most magnifies the Lord, and gives greatest glory to the One Creator, is, of all creatures,—not an angelic, but a human being.

Mary said, '*My soul.*' The word 'soul' is not one which can be applied to designate an angel. It signifies the ' spirit that is in man.' Angels are pure spirits; they are not souls. The difference between a pure spirit, or an angel, and a soul, is this: both are independent of matter, can exist apart from it, and so existing, perform all purely spiritual acts, such as those of memory, intellect, and will; can remember, understand and know, determine and love :—but a human soul, although it can exist apart from a material body, and although it has, so apart, the exercise of all its purely intellectual powers, forces, and faculties,

B

and that moreover in a higher degree, more unrestrainedly, more intensely, and more consciously then, in that moment when it is set free from the mortal and corruptible body — this body of death to which it is now united — although it then only begins really to understand its own nature, and the stretch and limit of its own capacities, and adequately to realise what it is to be a spirit — to possess a spiritual existence — to exercise spiritual faculties, and to live with a spiritual life — yet that disembodied spirit, even although full of grace, purified from every stain of sin, cleansed from the slightest soil of earth, nay, even after its entrance on the life invisible and immortal — after its admission to the eternal glory, and the undisturbed possession of the unseen, unheard-of, unconceived delights and joys and satisfactions of the beatific vision — even then that disembodied soul is still in an estate of imperfection. It is imperfect with the imperfection of a part; existing severed from that other part, union with which is necessary in order to the completeness of the whole; and it will not attain to its perfection until the day of the general resurrection, when that other part, its material body, shall be reformed from out those constituent elements into which, by decomposition, it has been resolved, reconstructed in accordance with a glorious, eternal, and divine idea, and renewed in all the perfection of which its nature is capable. Then shall the beatified soul not only put on that transformed body as a garment to cover its nakedness—not only enter into it as into a habitation and a home—but it shall assume it into its own unity, into the oneness of its own personal individuality; it shall be so intimately and indissolubly wedded to it that, in virtue of that eternal union, those two component parts of a human being, the human body and the human soul, shall thenceforth and for ever live with one human life, and act with one human operation.

The existence of a material being, so formed and organised by the processes of nature as that it should fittingly become a human body by the infusion into it of a human soul, was the moral cause inducing God to the creation, not only of a human soul, but of that particular human soul, with all its peculiar, personal, special, individual characteristics, qualities, properties, and perfections.

God does not simply create a soul—any kind of soul—to be united to and inform a body, without reference to that body; but He creates this particular soul in order to and with special and direct reference to this particular body, with a real relation and a special adaptation of one to the other, and in such wise that this body belongs to this soul—can claim it, possesses it by a right—a right of property, a title of dominion — can say strictly and with truth, ' *This* is *my* body.'

There exists now, at this moment, between the disembodied souls in purgatory and in paradise and the lifeless bodies in the grave—nay, between those souls and the constituent elements into which their bodies have been resolved—a real bond—so real that at the latter day this particular soul must necessarily be reunited to this particular body— to its own body—to identically that same body which it inhabited, informed, and possessed while here on earth.

Moreover, so intimate and so real is the union between soul and body — between this particular soul and this particular body—that, of the original divine intention, in the idea and purpose of the Creator from the beginning, that union was never to be dissolved. There was to be no death. Man had bestowed upon him the gift of immortality— the possibility of unending, uninterrupted human life, because the possibility of unending, uninterrupted union between soul and body. There was to be no purgatory, and no grave. Man was

to live for ever; and, his period of probation at
an end, to be translated alive from the paradise
on earth to the paradise of God.

The severance of the union, the dissolution of
the bond, the divorce of soul and body, was the
consequence of sin : 'The wages of sin is death.'
'By man sin entered into the world, and death by
sin; and so death passed upon all men, for that
all have sinned.' It was the Divine decree : 'In
the day that thou sinnest thou shalt die.' Henceforth—from the moment of the first human transgression of the Divine law — there was not only
heaven and earth, a temporary pilgrimage and
an eternal home—there was a hell for fallen man
as for rebel angels. There was a grave, in which
should be buried the disembodied souls, as well
as a grave into which should be cast the lifeless
bodies of the damned. Sin had thwarted the
Divine intention of an everlasting union between
soul and body—had rendered an impossibility the
original design of the Creator. Sin begot death;
and death begot hell and the grave.

But then appeared the goodness and mercy and
long-suffering of our God, in the decree and creation of a purgatory, to endure till time should be
no more, and, on the latter day of time, a resurrection from the dead. The sin-stained body and

the sin-stained soul were alike to be buried, yet buried but for a season. The one would be searched and cleansed by the purifying flames, the other would pass through the alembic of the grave; and both should be reunited in the unity and perfection of renewed and transformed and glorified human beings.

Such was the divine design with regard to, such the history and such the destiny of the human soul.

And now compare with a human soul an angel or pure spirit. Such a spirit not only has no parts, but it is not and cannot be a part of any whole. It is perfect and complete in its own singleness; it neither desires, requires, nor is capable of union with a body.

Angels, it is true, have appeared in human form; and those forms were not merely spectral appearances, mere phantoms or phenomena, but material frames, that could be seen and touched and handled; that could utter words and perform organic acts—could partake of that repast that Sara prepared in her tent on the plains of Mambre, and that Abraham served as he stood by them under the tree.

They were bodies, but they were not *their* bodies. The angel and that body did not form together one human being. Neither was it an incarnation of an angelic being. There were not two natures, an angelic and a human, subsisting in the unity of one angelic person. The angel and that body were not united in the oneness of one life; those organic acts did not proceed from one principle, and did not combine in one operation. The angel was merely clothed with that human body; dwelt and energised within it, in like manner as a man clothes himself with a garment. That body was extrinsic to the angel, and not part of himself; he assumed it for a time, used it for a particular purpose; and when that time was at an end, and that purpose was served, the usefulness to him of that body was gone, and he laid it aside as that for which he had no longer need. For an angel to be perpetually confined within the limits of a material body would be as much an imperfection as it would be an imperfection for a human soul perpetually to act and exist apart from that body which belongs to it, and is its own.

Now that intellectual being which is greatest in the scale of beings, and which most magnifies the Lord, is,—not a pure spirit, not an angel, but a human soul.

As to the relative superiority of these two, an angel and a human soul, we read in Holy Scrip-

ture that, at the first, God made man 'a little
lower than the angels;' and it is true that, looking
merely to the nature of each in the abstract, an
angel is greater than a man in the scale of creatures, and consequently can give to God a higher
worship and a greater glory.

But if we look to the destiny, and to the history of man, which manifests and fulfils that destiny — to the Incarnation of the Eternal Word,
whereby it was accomplished — to the creation of
that second human family of the sons of God —
the children begotten of the Second Adam and
His mystic Bride — the family of the redeemed
built up out of the ruins of the family of the fallen
—that great multitude gathered out of every kindred, and nation, and people, and tongue, redeemed
and cleansed by the Precious Blood—if we look to
the dignity of the human race, as it is ennobled
by the fact that the God-Man is consubstantial
with the sons of Adam, even in the order of nature, and according to the flesh; and to the farther
fact that in the supernatural order they are each
in turn individually made consubstantial with Him
—made one flesh and blood with their Redeemer
and their God through and by means of the Blessed
Sacrament—then we see the force and significance
and meaning of those words of the Psalmist quoted

in the Epistle to the Hebrews, and applied by the Apostle of the Gentiles primarily, indeed, to the Second Adam; but really, albeit secondarily and consequently, to all His children. 'What is man, that Thou art mindful of him, or the son of man, that Thou visitest him? Thou hast made him a a little lower than the angels; Thou hast crowned him with glory and honour, and hast set him over the works of Thy hands. Thou hast subjected all things under his feet. He took hold not of the nature of angels, but of the seed of Abraham.'

In virtue of our twofold consubstantiality, and of our moral identity with Him by our existence and life in the One mystical Body, His superiority over the angelic hierarchies extends also to us, the members of that His Body—to us, who are one with Him, and whose life is hid with Christ in God—to us, who have put on Christ, and are found in Him. Hence, said He, 'the glory that Thou hast given Me I have given them.' In this sense, then, by our incorporation into Christ, we men are higher than the angels.

But there was another reason, taken from the nature of his being, which qualified and adapted man for a position of superiority in the worship of his Maker. It was this: 'Man is,' says Plato, 'a microcosm of creation.' In the unity of his own individuality subsist the two opposite poles of being, the material and the spiritual. In man energise all the forms of life, organic and spiritual—the vegetative, the sensitive, and the intellective. Man, therefore, was fitted by the nature of his being to become the high-priest of creation.

But this was not to be till the fulness of time had come. For four thousand years the angels held their place of superiority, and man acknowledged the validity of their title and the justice of their claim. That same Abraham of whom we have spoken, as soon as he saw the three angels approaching him as he sat in his tent-door in the heat of the day, ran to meet them, and adored down to the ground. The parents of Samson, when they understood that he whom they saw ascending heavenwards in the flames of the altar was an angel of the Lord, fell flat on the ground. Daniel also, that man of desires, a prophet of God, and one familiar with visions and supernatural manifestations, when he saw Gabriel, fell on his face trembling.

But in the moment of the Immaculate Conception, the angels had a Human Queen; and on the day of the Annunciation, Gabriel—*Fortitudo Dei*, 'the Strength of God'—a Prince among the angels—'the angel who stands in the presence of

God'—acknowledged her royalty, abased himself before her, and realised himself as nothing in her presence.

When, by His creative omnipotence, the Triune God called the soul of Mary out of nothingness into existence, it was as yet the masterpiece of all His works, the greatest and most royal of all spiritual beings; its capacities unfathomed, as they were unsurpassed, by any created intelligence. The angels, beholding it, were lost in awe and reverence at its merely natural perfections, at its perfections as a creature, as a human soul. It exceeded and excelled not only those of any individual angel, or of any individual soul of man that had ever existed, but those also of all angels and of all human souls together.

But this was merely its natural and its lowest perfection. It was a perfection that had its perfection in being a capacity for an ulterior perfection, for a supernatural perfection,—a perfection above all the perfections of its nature, and beyond all its exigencies.

Mary's soul was not merely a marvel of natural beauty, a miracle of creative wisdom and power. It was in that moment of its creation—in the first instant of its existence—charged with sanctifying grace. This added to it a supernatural lustre and radiance, a beauty and brilliance, a loveableness and attractiveness, which not merely caused God to gaze upon it with complacency and love and joy, but impelled Him to desire it; to long to enter into and possess and enjoy it; to have it and hold it as His own; to dwell and to reign within it without a rival. It was the coveted home, the most royal residence, the chiefest palace of the Blessed Trinity. 'The rushing of the river of grace made glad the City of God.' Of Mary's soul God could say: 'This is My rest for ever; here will I dwell, for I have a delight therein.'

But again : it was not merely *passively* that in her Immaculate Conception Mary magnified the Lord; not merely as being a resplendent manifestation of His wisdom and power—a clear, unspotted, unclouded mirror of the Divine perfections; it was not as a mere inert and inactive, albeit glorious, royal, peerless creature, but *actively*; by an exertion of her own faculties; by an exercise of her intellect and her will; and it was thus especially that she magnified the Lord.

But what mean we by the word '*magnify*'? It means literally to make great; to add to one's greatness; to increase one's glory, and so to give to one something which he had not before. But how can this apply to the great God, the God of glory

—to Him in regard of Whom the ideas of increase and diminution, of addition and subtraction, are repugnant, inconsistent, and incompatible? And how, moreover, can a creature be said to magnify its Creator—a creature who, by the very fact of its being a creature, not only has nothing, but is nothing, apart from its Creator; who owes all it is and has to Him? *Quid habes, quod non accepisti?*—'what have you that you have not received?'

And yet it is a revealed truth—certain with the certainty of divine faith—that the creature can and does magnify its Creator, add to His greatness, increase His glory, and give to Him something which, without that creature, and, apart from an act of that creature's will, He would not have. The explanation is this. A twofold glory pertains to God—an *essential* glory and an *accidental* glory. His *Essential* Glory is that which of necessity belongs to Him, without which He would not be God, and in order to which He is absolutely self-sufficing. This Essential Glory is the result and issue of the processes of His own inner life. He has His Beatitude and His Glory in the contemplation and love of Himself, of His own Essence and Being, as it is the infinitely True and the infinitely Good. He is self-sufficing in order to His own glory, as He is self-sufficing in order to His own existence. He has no cause of that existence, and this glory also He does not derive from another. ' All my goods,' says the Psalmist, ' are nothing unto Thee.'

But besides this *Essential* Glory, He has also an *accidental* glory, which it is possible for Him to receive from His own creatures, from every work of His hands; but above all, and beyond all, from His intelligent and rational creatures. The water which runs downhill instead of upwards, and which finds its level; the waves of the sea in their ebb and flow, and in the succession of their tides; the sun and the moon in their rising and in their setting; the stars in their courses—one and all praise and magnify the Lord by their natural obedience to those physical laws which He has ordained them. The grass of the field, the flowers which adorn and beautify the earth, the trees which grow thereon, magnify the Lord by living according to the laws of that life which He has bestowed upon them. The beasts of the earth, the birds of the air, and the fishes of the sea magnify the Lord by following those instincts which He has implanted within them.

They one and all magnify, each after its manner, and according to the mode of its own specific or individual being. But theirs is an inferior worship. It does not satisfy, much less satiate God. It is good and sufficient and adequate of its kind; but He desires more than the natural and necessary worship of the inanimate and the irrational. And, moreover, it has in it no merit; for they have no freedom of will; they cannot offer, for they cannot refuse. They live and act not by choice and purpose, but by a necessity of their nature; and they are incapable therefore of either reward or punishment.

But His intelligent creatures, human and angelic, have a higher existence and a nobler nature, more nearly approaching His own. His image is more sharply and adequately stamped upon them. They are clearer mirrors of His own spiritual perfections. They possess life; but not mere life, not only life in its lower form, the organic, but in its highest form, the spiritual and intellective. They can know and will; they can apprehend and understand; they can purpose and resolve and determine. Moreover, their spiritual faculties of intellect and will tend like His, till they rest in possession of the true and the good. To these they naturally tend, but not by a natural necessity. They have another God-like gift—absolute freedom of the will. They can will to reject, as they can will to embrace the truth. They can will to refuse, as they can will to choose and cleave to the good. They can will their own perfection and consequent glory, and they can equally will their own distortion and consequent ruin. They can will their Maker's glory or His dishonour; for that glory and their perfection are identified, as is His injury and their loss. By the selfsame process whereby they perfect themselves, they glorify Him; and by the selfsame process whereby they glorify Him, they perfect themselves as they are spiritual beings.

Hence, in order to these two ends, His glory and their perfection, the Allwise and Loving Creator has given to His intelligent and rational creatures alike a revelation and a law; a Revelation the embracing of which, as His Truth, will perfect their understandings; and a Law, submission to which, as it is divine, will perfect their wills. Moreover, besides this external revelation and law, He has given them those internal graces, those participations of the Divine nature, whereby they are enabled to perform those two supernatural acts of faith and obedience. He has given them the grace of illumination and the grace of inspiration: the one, enlightening the understanding, that it may see; the other, subduing the will, that it may subject itself and obey. He has given them, in a word, the grace of the light of Divine faith, and the grace of the flame of Divine charity.

Now those graces were bestowed upon our Blessed Lady in her Immaculate Conception, in the first instant of her human existence, in the first moment in which she lived with a human life.

Of us, as of all the children of the first Adam, two things are true. First, that we are conceived in iniquity, and brought forth in sin; and secondly, that even after we have received the gift of sanctifying grace—that gift of spiritual light and life which dispels the darkness and destroys the death of our original sin—after we have been born again by the Sacrament of the new birth, regenerated by Holy Baptism, transferred from the family of the fallen into the family of the redeemed—after we have put off the old Adam and put on the New; dissolved our spiritual connection with the first man, who is of the earth earthy, and entered into a spiritual oneness with the Second Man, the Lord from heaven; after the hateful stain left by the original transgression has been removed from our souls by the immaculate lustre of our first habitual grace—even then something is lacking to us which will only come with our increase in age and stature, with the lapse of time and the progress of the years. We as yet lack *actual* graces, and that simply for this reason, that as yet we are incapable of them.

Our souls inhabit and inform our infant bodies; and in virtue of this, those bodies live with a human life. Our souls within those bodies are complete as to their essence, and really possess all their faculties; but those faculties are dormant. We have not as yet their use and exercise; there is no energy of the intellectual as of the organic life. There will be a dawn of reason; and the moment is as yet in the future, when the will shall for the first time act intelligently. As yet we cannot think and know and understand, much less purpose, and determine, and resolve, and will. We are not as yet responsible for our acts. What we do is not morally imputable to us. We have neither merit nor demerit; we deserve no praise, and we incur no blame. There is no foundation for reward, and there is none for punishment.

We, in our infant life, are incapable of human acts, and therefore we are incapable of and we need no *actual* graces — those graces which are given to us in order that the human acts of our human will, instructed by our human intellect, with its human knowledge, should be not merely natural, but supernatural; not merely deserving of an earthly reward, but meritorious of the life eternal in the supernatural Vision of God.

But it was otherwise with Mary. She never for a moment lived with a human organic life that she did not live also with a human intellective life.

As with the angels and with Adam, in the first instant of their creation, so with the Queen of angels and the Mother of men. In the first instant of her human existence, she had the full and perfect use and the free exercise of her intellectual faculties. There was for her an anticipation of the dawn of reason and of will. She never lived that she did not also think, and understand, and know, and purpose, and determine, and resolve, and will.

In the selfsame moment there was also present to her mind a revelation of Divine truth, and a manifestation of the Divine law. She knew the Divine will. It was proposed to her as the rule and measure of her own.

And finally, and in order that her will might be responsive—that it should bend beneath the pressure of the Divine Will, that the two should thrill in unison—there was, over and above her habitual grace, and because of that grace, which gives to all who possess it a real right and indefeasible title to actual graces *in tempore opportuno,* in time of need — bestowed upon Mary a gift of actual graces, equal to her wants. Aided by those graces, her illuminated understanding embraced and held fast that infused revelation of Divine truth; and her sanctified will tended towards, stretched out to, united and wedded itself to, and clave steadfastly to the Divine Will, as manifested to her by that law of which her Maker had given her this preternatural knowledge.

Why should I attempt to prove this? How can we conceive it otherwise? Can we conceive that perfections which God bestowed upon the first man and the first woman, as well as upon the angels, in the first moment of their creation, should be denied to the Queen of the angels, and the spiritual Mother of mankind, in the first moment of her being? Adam possessed, Eve possessed, the lowest of the angels possessed, in the first moment of their being, the use and exercise of all their faculties, the gift of sanctifying grace, as well as of those actual graces to which it gives a right, and of which they then had need, along with a knowledge of the Triune God, and a manifestation of His law. Would those gifts have been denied by the Eternal Father to His queenliest Daughter, by the Only-begotten to His chosen Mother, by the Holy Ghost to His destined Spouse? Why, even the Baptist was sanctified in the womb, recognised, adored, and rejoiced while yet unborn. Is Mary less, and are her privileges no more?

In the first moment of her human existence, she made a magnificent act of divine faith, another of divine hope, and a third of divine charity. Her whole soul adored its Maker with an unparalleled and peerless act of adoration. Her words in after days but gave expression to what she did in the dawn of her existence. '*Magnificat anima mea Dominum*,'—'My soul doth magnify the Lord.'

Yes; she truly magnified the Lord. Never before, by angel or by child of Adam, had their common Lord been so adequately magnified as by the unborn Mary. Never before had He been magnified by so grand, so glorious, so perfect, so peerless a creature; and never before by so grand, so glorious, so perfect, and so peerless an act of adoration.

All the adoration of the angels, and all the adorations of men for centuries of years, were not in their united sum equal to that one, that first adoration of the Immaculate Mary.

Practically, as well as speculatively, Mary recognised and acknowledged the Triune God, in the moment of her creation, to be *the* Lord and *her*

Lord—to have a right of sovereignty and dominion over her, of property and possession in her.

What this implies and includes, I reserve till I speak of her humility, the solid, deep-laid foundation of all her greatness. Suffice it to say now, that she perfectly and adequately realised her end, the final cause of her existence, the reason of her being—to know, to love, and to serve her Maker. And in the freedom of her will, by the aid of her grace, she made a purpose and resolution then, which endured throughout the entire term of her mortal sojourn, and increased and intensified with the passing days of the years of her life on earth— to perfect herself by that knowledge and that love, and, thus perfected, to magnify her Maker by that service.

Therefore it is, in virtue of that perseverance even until death, that she is now exalted far above principalities and powers, that she is crowned with glory and honour, and seated on the Second Throne, next to the King, and at the King's Right Hand. There enthroned in royalty above the subject angels, she leads and presents to God the Magnificat of the sons of men; of all who, by grace, have become her children, and can say with her in spirit and in truth, 'My soul doth magnify the Lord.'

II.

Exultavit spiritus meus.
My spirit hath rejoiced. *St. Luke* i. 47.

HAVING considered the word 'soul,' what it expresses and what is implied in it, we come now to consider the word '*spirit*.' Mary said, 'My spirit hath rejoiced,' and 'My soul doth magnify.' What is the reason for this difference? for a reason we must suppose, when we remember that the words were uttered by Mary, and that they were dictated by the inspiration of the Holy Ghost.

Her use of the word '*soul*' was to signify the entirety of her worship and adoration, wherewith she magnified the Lord. It was the service of her whole human being, of all her emotions, affections, and feelings, as well as of her intellect and will.

But now she uses the word '*spirit*,' and that to show the nature and character of her rejoicing; that it was not a mere, and was not always an affective or emotional joy, but an intellectual and supernatural rejoicing.

The human **soul**, the spirit **that** is in man, has all the powers and faculties that **an** angel, a pure spirit, has; **but it has more;** and **therefore** it is called a *soul*, and not merely a *spirit*. **When we** speak of all those faculties, and mean **to express** them, then **we speak** of it as a *soul*. When, on the contrary, **we speak** of those faculties only which it has in common with the angels—the faculties of memory, of intellect, and of will—then we speak of it as a *spirit*.

Those latter faculties are sometimes, although not in strictness and with accuracy, spoken of as constituting the *higher soul;* while the other faculties— the emotions, affections, feelings, passions, and appetites—are spoken of as constituting the *lower soul,* I say, not with strict accuracy, for the soul is one. There is but one soul in man, and those are all faculties of one and the selfsame soul; but we speak as if it were otherwise, in order to express the fact, that the two sets of faculties may be in opposition the one to the other—the higher faculties tending in one direction, and the lower faculties drawn in another.

The lower faculties are ordained by their Creator in order to the exercise of the higher; and they are necessary for this exercise, in our present state of existence. According to the original intention of the Creator, and before the fall which frustrated that intention, the two sets of faculties were in perfect harmony; the lower was in a state of perfect subordination to the higher; the sensitive did service to the intellective, the flesh was subdued to the spirit. But now since the fall, and under the reign of concupiscence which it introduced, the lower faculties are often drawn earthwards, even while the higher faculties tend towards heaven.

Let us look for a moment at the original Divine idea.

According to it, man was to be immortal. There was to be no dissolution of the bond that bound together soul and body in the oneness of one human life. Because immortal, he was to be also impassible. There was to be none of that physical suffering which precedes and issues in death. Old age would indeed come upon him, but without aught of senility, decrepitude, or decay. There was in him no seed of disease, no intrinsic principle of dissolution.

And as with the body, so also with the soul of man. As there was to be no physical, so also there was to be no mental suffering; no agonies of perplexity and doubt; none of that dejection and despondency which culminates in despair; no timidity and fear; no sadness and sorrow; no remorse for the past, no grief for the present, and no anxiety and foreboding for the future. He had the gift of felicity; and its result was calm and tranquillity of soul, and joy and peace.

Moreover, of the original Divine intention, there was to be no cloud of ignorance to overshadow and enshroud his soul like a dreary mist, or a dismal haze that intercepts the glad sunshine. His understanding was to be undarkened, and to possess the gift of knowledge—not that knowledge which we gain by study, and acquire by labour and toil, by the travail of the weary brain; but a God-given, infused knowledge, shed into the soul by its Maker.

But this beautiful, bountiful, munificent Divine ideal was destroyed by the will of man. He thwarted the creative intention of his Maker. He transgressed the Divine law; and in virtue of that transgression death entered into the world, and with death the suffering that precedes it—the pain and disease, the physical torture, and the agonies that excruciate the corruptible body.

Added to these, and in their train, came agony of soul, that mental torture that transcends all tortures of the flesh; there came perplexity and doubt, disquiet and unrest and remorse of conscience, melancholy brooding over present evils, and fearful forebodings as to what the veiled future might have in store. Henceforth also men's understandings were darkened, their wills were depraved, and their memories were at the first a blank. They had sinned through the senses, through the seeing of the eye, and the hearing of the ear, and henceforth their spirits were to be in subjection to their senses. They were to have no knowledge in their understandings, no conceptions in their memories that did not enter by the avenue of the senses. All their knowledge of the outer world, and of the Creator of that world, was to be come by in this way.

Even that supernatural knowledge which constitutes the object of Divine faith was to be acquired by this method and in this manner: 'faith cometh by hearing.'

The truths of faith would be apprehended and embraced by the intellect, and would find therein their residence and home; but they would not be mere passive indwellers. Their existence there would not be inactive and inert. They would be mainsprings and motive powers; they would act upon and influence the will. The intellect would be *practical* as well as speculative; and as such it would be termed and become the *conscience;* and then the will, operating and acting in obedience to the dictates of the reason, would regain its old supremacy, and exercise dominion over the whole sensitive nature, over all the inferior powers and faculties of soul and body.

But even then, after the reëstablishment of the habitual dominion of the will over the inferior faculties, that dominion would be exercised over them not as over obedient servants, as in the days of primeval, unfallen innocence; it would be exercised over them as over subjugated rebels and vanquished enemies, ever inclined to insubordination, and on the alert for an opportunity of revolt.

This is the case with all the redeemed and regenerate. It is so even with the Saints on earth; nay, even with the Apostles of Jesus Christ. It was so with that man of iron will, that vessel of election, the self-subjugated Apostle of the Gentiles. He had to fight for the dominion, and to struggle for the mastery; and such was the strength of his enemies, that he seems to tremble for the issue of the contest. He tells us of the law in his members fighting against the law of his mind, and captivating him in the law of sin. He says he is delighted with the law of God, according to the inward man; but 'when I have a will to do good, evil is present with me.' 'The good which I will,

I do not; but the evil which I will not, that I do.'
He tells us in another place of 'the sting in his
flesh,' 'the messenger of Satan' given him to buffet
him; and he declares his necessity of keeping
under his body, and bringing it into subjection, lest
he who had preached to others should himself become a castaway.

The Apostle refers to the *fomes peccati*, that
fuel of sin, which remains in order to their probation, even in those who have had 'power to
become the sons of God,' and 'partakers of the
Divine Nature;' that proneness, and promptitude,
and facility, and inclination towards the objects of
sense which causes the emotions, and feelings, and
affections, and appetites, and passions to anticipate
the judgments of the illuminated reason, and to
pervert the will from obedience to its dictates. The
energy of this language of St. Paul, provoked by
the vehemence of his struggle, is such that he goes
so far as to call this *fomes* sin. Not that it is
really and truly, morally and culpably, sin; but, as
the Fathers of Trent explain his words, inasmuch
as it proceeds from sin and inclines to sin. It is
entailed upon us by the original transgression, and
it is the prolific parent of actual sins.

One and one only of the children of Adam was
exempt from this consequence of his fall. It was

she on whose immaculate soul the stain of his transgression never for an instant lay. She had to fight against the world and against the devil, as he had; but she had not, like him, after he had lost his innocence, to fight against the flesh. There was in her no responsive voice from within to temptations from without. There was no household foe, no traitor in the fortress of the City of our God. But although she was free from sin, and from the *fomes* of sin; although she was, like the first mother of all living, endowed with the preternatural gift of immortality, there being in her no intrinsic principle of dissolution, and no seed of disease; although she enjoyed impassibility, or freedom from all liability to physical suffering from any intrinsic cause, so that, for instance, she had not to bear the curse of Eve, and endure the pangs of travail,—and old age when it came upon her would not bring in its train aught of decrepitude or decay; although she possessed an infused gift of knowledge that preserved her from the defect of ignorance and the infirmity of error, yet a shadow of the fall lay on Mary:—Mary was amenable to suffering. And this was no disparagement to her prerogatives, no derogation from her perfections, for the selfsame shadow lay on her Divine Son.

There is no sin and no shame in suffering.

True, it is the result and issue of sin. It is a punishment, and punishment supposes sin. It is a satisfaction, and satisfaction supposes an offence. But the satisfaction may be offered, and the punishment may be endured, by one for another, by the innocent for the guilty, by the just for the sinner.

Hence Isaias prophesied of the future Son of Mary that He was to be 'a Man of sorrows, and acquainted with infirmity;' that He was to 'bear our infirmities' and 'carry our sorrows;' that He was to be 'wounded for our iniquities' and 'bruised for our sins;' that the chastisement of our peace 'was to be upon Him,' and that by His 'bruises we should be healed.' The Lord was 'to lay upon Him the iniquity of us all:' 'for the wickedness of My people,' said the Almighty, 'have I struck Him.'

Of Him also St. Paul says: 'We have not an High - priest who cannot have compassion upon our infirmities, but one tempted in all things like as we are, without sin.'

Suffering was a law of the Incarnation. That the Incarnate Word might redeem and satisfy, it became Him to suffer. If He was to satisfy the Justice of the offended God, and redeem the guilty race that through sin lay under captivity and bondage, He must become the Suffering God. Hence

His own words to Cleophas: 'Ought not Christ to have suffered, *and so* to enter into His glory?'

St. Peter, in his discourse to the people who gathered around him in Solomon's porch, after his miraculous healing of the lame man, declared that the sufferings of Christ were the fulfilment of those things which God before had showed by the mouth of all the prophets.

Again, the argument of St. Paul, when for three Sabbath days he reasoned with the Jews in their synagogue at Thessalonica out of the Scriptures, was this:—that the Christ was to suffer, and to rise again from the dead. This, to use his own words, he 'declared and insinuated.' He preached it in express words, and it was also the implicit argument that underlay his entire doctrine.

The same Apostle, in presence of the King Agrippa and Bernice, standing before the tribunal of the governor Festus in the hall of audience at Cesarea, and in the hearing of the tribunes and principal men of the city, said that,—aided by the help of God, he witnessed both to small and great, saying no other things than those which the prophets and Moses did say should come to pass, that Christ should suffer.

If, then, it became Christ to suffer, so does it also become all the members of His mystical Body, all who are one with Him in the oneness of its one mystical life; nay! and to suffer all the more in proportion as their life is 'hid with Christ in God.'

And this was the reason why it became Mary to suffer. Suffering has a threefold end. It may be vindictive, it may be remedial, and it may be simply unitive. In her case, it could be neither vindictive nor remedial. It could not be vindictive, for in her there was no offence to punish. It could not be remedial, for in her there was no disease to remedy, and no stain to cleanse. Mary's sufferings were therefore unitive. God permitted and inflicted them in order to conform her to the image of her suffering Son, that in all things she might be made like unto Him. She was taken up into the oneness of His life more fully and more closely than any other created being; but suffering was a mode identified with that life; and therefore Mary's life was necessarily a life of suffering. It became Mary to suffer, and so to enter into her glory.

It is of supreme importance that we should adequately apprehend the *reality* of the sufferings of our Divine Lord. He really suffered the privations and hardships of Bethlehem and Nazareth and the Nile. He really suffered the sickening pangs of hunger, and the burning fever of unslaked

D

thirst, after the forty days' fast in the wilderness of Quarentana. He was really fatigued and footsore when He rested from His journey on the parapet of Jacob's well, by the city of Sichar in Samaria. He was really weary when He slept in the stern of Peter's boat on the Sea of Galilee. He shed real tears of real human sorrow at the grave of Lazarus of Bethania, His friend and the brother of His friends; and again on the slope of Olivet, as He beheld across the valley the beloved but doomed city—His own Jerusalem in her stately beauty, and with all her sacred associations—and thought of the coming day of her visitation which she knew not. He really feared, and was amazed and very heavy, as He really agonised in the Garden of Gethsemani. His—'Father, if it be possible, let this chalice pass from Me'—was nature's assertion of its repugnance to suffering. Those words expressed what in His lower soul He really felt—the recoil of His lower sensitive nature from pain and shame, from suffering and sorrow, from agony and death. He really felt the betrayal of Judas and the denial of Peter and the ungenerous flight of the Apostles. He really suffered as from the Cross He looked down upon the steadfast sorrow of the virginal Disciple, on the wild passionate grief of the Magdalen, and on the broken heart of Mary. He really felt the bodily pain, the physical torture, of the stripes at the pillar, of the blows in the guard-house, and of the nailing and suspension on the Cross. He felt as really as and all that an ordinary man would have felt; and this suffering, in its almost unbearable reality, was only the foundation of His Passion; for that Passion is to be measured in its intensity, not by the three hours of its continuance, but to be multiplied by the number of the entire human race; beginning with the soul of Adam, and including the last soul created on the last day of time. Nay! it is to be multiplied again by the number of mortal sins which every individual of that race should perpetrate. In a word, His sufferings were not single. They were manifold as the number of men to be redeemed, and of mortal sins to expiate.

Hence the mournful words of Jeremias, in the Lamentation which the Church makes her own, as she contemplates the mysteries of the Passion: 'O all ye that pass by the way, attend, and see if there be any sorrow like unto My sorrow!'

And now,—with the same reality wherewith the sorrows and the sufferings of Jesus were real, were the sufferings and sorrows of Mary also real. As His Humanity, and the feelings connatural to that Humanity, were not consumed in the furnace of

His Divinity, so neither were hers in the furnace of her unparalleled graces.

But this Divinity and those graces — those created participations of that Divine nature—were the sources and fountains of spiritual joy to both Jesus and Mary. In the midst of their tribulations, amid the acutest agonies of their most overwhelming sorrows, in the depths of their unconceived and unutterable woe, Jesus and Mary could both say, and say with truth, '*Exultat spiritus meus,*'—'My spirit doth rejoice.' Not even in the moment of His greatest trial, during the dereliction of the Eternal Father, and that darkness of His soul which accompanied the noon-day darkness of the eclipse on Calvary, the desolation that wrung from Him the exceeding bitter cry, 'My God, My God, why hast Thou forsaken Me?'—not even then was the human soul of Jesus deprived of its spiritual joy.

From the first moment of His conception, His created human soul enjoyed the Beatific Vision of the Triune God. Once bestowed, this vision never left Him; for the gifts of God are without repentance. Even death, which, severing the union between soul and body, deprived Him of His human life, did not deprive Him of that Vision. But its *effects* might be restrained; and they were re-

strained during the days of His earthly sojourn,
and this that He might be passible and mortal,
that He might be able to suffer and die, and so
merit and redeem, propitiate and atone. The
ordinary, the normal, effect of the Beatific Vision
would have been to extend that glory which it
bestowed upon His soul to the body which that
soul inhabited and informed. But this normal
effect was restrained; and for that unselfish reason, for the sake of 'us men and for our salvation.'
Once only do we read that He allowed the glory
of His soul to have its natural course; and that
was on the day of His Transfiguration on the summit of Thabor, that transfiguration which was the
prelude of His humiliation on the hill-top of Calvary. Then He manifested forth His glory that
His Disciples might believe in Him.

Now just as He restrained His Beatific Glory
from extending itself to His Sacred Body, so could
He also restrain His Beatific Joy from extending
itself to and permeating those emotions, affections,
feelings, and sensitive appetites which together
form what we have called the 'lower soul;' and
this in order that in and through them He might
suffer whatever they are capable of suffering.

But His higher soul, His intellective faculties,
His mind and will, that Beatific Vision, its glory

and its joy, never for a moment deserted. That soul with those faculties was in His darkest hour inundated and inebriated by the unseen, unheard of, and unconceived delights and joys and satisfactions of the Beatific Vision.

And as it was with Jesus, so also was it with Mary in her measure. There was not one of her sorrowful mysteries that was not also a mystery of joy, and of which she could not say, '*Exultavit spiritus meus*,'—'My spirit hath rejoiced.'

It seems at first sight a strange thing to say, but it is as strictly true as strange, that the very first of her joyful mysteries was a mystery of sorrow. Her consent at the Annunciation, when Gabriel conveyed to her the Divine message which solicited it, was a heroic act, transcending in its heroicity all the sufferings and death struggles of all the martyrs.

To the superficial reader of the sacred narrative this does not appear, for it lies beneath the surface. It does not occur to him that there was required a grace to elicit the words whereby she signified her consent, and gave effect to the decree of the Incarnation. '*Fiat mihi secundum verbum Tuum*,'—'Be it done to me according to Thy word,'—to him seem easy words to say, and said in obedience to the most natural of natural impulses.

Men do not naturally shrink from and refuse honour and glory. These are the objects of their desire, of their covetousness and ambition. For these they scheme, and strive, and struggle, and make sacrifices. Why, then, should Mary hesitate? There was offered to her, there was placed within her reach, the greatest honour that the Creator could bestow upon any creature, and, as its consequence, the greatest glory that a creature could possibly receive—the peerless privilege and the unparalleled prerogatives that must of necessity attach to the office and dignity of Mother of God.

Yes; but there was another aspect of that office. She was to be the Mother of God, but of the suffering God, the rejected God, the despised God, the betrayed God, the denied God, the forsaken God, the reviled and blasphemed God, the scourged God, the crucified God.

All that Isaias and the other prophets had said of Him, and with which she was familiar from her study of the Hebrew Scriptures during the days of her sojourn within the Temple cloister, was present to her mind at that moment; and her woman's heart, along with her gift of wisdom, told her that the Mother of God must be a mother of sorrows; that what He endured in His Body she, in virtue of her mother's sympathy and compassion, must endure also in her soul. She counted the cost, and knew to what her consent committed her. She was not dazzled by the brilliance of the joyful and glorious aspect of the Divine maternity, so as to make her insensible and callous and indifferent to and forget the other. Nay, more; the brilliance of the prospect in the future, when all should have been accomplished, when she should have passed with Him, side by side and hand in hand, through the fathomless sea of suffering, and stood at the last on the farther shore—this was not that which determined her will, and gave her courage and nerve and strength to accept the office, and resolve to undergo the ordeal that it entailed. No; her own words give us the motive, the mainspring of her consent: 'Be it done to me according to Thy word.' It was the Divine word, the expression to her of the Divine will; and that will was the rule of her actions and the law of her life. She wedded her will to the will of her Maker by an act of superhuman charity; and on the instant the Holy Ghost, the hypostatic Will of God, the personal Love of the Father and of the Son, descended and overshadowed her; and the Incarnate Word dwelt within His chosen created home.

The consubstantial Son of the Eternal Father

was Son of Man, and consubstantial with the human race. The Virgin was a mother; and the joy of her maternity had possession of her soul. All that a mother feels she felt, in its highest and in its purest, in its intensest and most entrancing form. And yet the joy of her maternity was not the greatest of her joys. It is a joy which is rather of the lower than of the higher soul—which more belongs to the emotions and feelings and affections than to the strictly intellective faculties. True it is that in her maternal joy they also had their share. She apprehended and realised in mind and understanding, by intelligence and reason, what she felt in her mother's heart.

Yet still her merely maternal joy was not her greatest.

To us it seems so, and to us the other appears, in comparison of this, transcendental and unreal. We, in the weakness of our faith, and in the coldness of our love, incline to cry with the woman in the crowd, who, seeing and hearing Him, lifted up her voice and said, '*Beatus venter qui Te portavit, et beata ubera quæ Tu suxisti.*' But He, her Son, the Incarnate Wisdom, said, 'Yea, rather blessed are they who hear the word of God, and keep it.'

He was not comparing those who keep His

commandments, and do His will, and so testify
their love, with Mary His Mother, and to her disparagement. He was comparing Mary under one
aspect with the same Mary under another. He
was showing that to her it was a greater glory, a
greater blessedness, and a greater joy to have her
will vibrating in unison with her Maker's, than
to have given to the Eternal Word a body from
the fountains of her blood. As with Him, so with
her: 'My meat and drink is to do the will of my
Father Who is in heaven.'

It was this, her spiritual joy, that never for-
sook her, that ever sustained her. Repulsed from
door to door, through the streets of Bethlehem,
in the chill December night: '*It is His will.*'
Toiling across the barren sands, beneath a burning sun, a fugitive from the sword of the ruthless
Herod, a stranger among the idolaters of Egypt:
'*It is His will.*' Deprived of the society of the
good and gentle, the cultured and refined; cut off
from the friendship of such as became her royal
lineage, a dweller among the evil and the fro-
ward, among the savage boors of ill-famed Nazareth: '*It is His will.*' Following the blood-stained
footsteps of her Son along the way of the Cross,
and gazing on His agonies: '*It is His will.*' Childless and desolate at the third hour: still '*It is His*

will.' The desolation of her childlessness was the culmination of her sorrows. All was accomplished; and Mary was alone. Her solitude in her sorrow was the crown of her sorrows. High rank and unshared dignity have their drawbacks and their disadvantages: they isolate their possessor, and deprive him of the sympathy of those beneath him. Mary stood utterly alone. No one could apprehend, much less appreciate in its reality, her sorrow. John, with his new sonship and office of her guardian, and Magdalene, with her burning love, stronger than death, were alike powerless to fathom the sea of her suffering, and still less to enter with her into its depths. There was but one Mother of God; and no one save that Mother could understand or share that mother's sorrows. And yet even now—*Exultavit spiritus meus.*

Now what was the secret source of this perpetual joy of Mary? It was nothing of a kind peculiar to herself, but something common to us all—to you and to me. It was simply the result of her exercise of three graces, which the Holy Ghost bestowed upon her, and in which we also have our share. Her joy was the issue and offspring of her faith, her hope, and her charity. The 'fruit of the Spirit is joy and peace.' There is a 'joy and peace in believing.' It is the rest and quiet, the tranquillity and calm, the repose of a soul no longer agitated by perplexity and doubt and unbelief, but peaceful in its possession of absolute truth, proposed to it by a Divine authority, accepted with entire submission, and held with absolute certainty. There is also the peace of a conscience void of offence towards God and towards man—the consciousness that not the shadow of a cloud or a coldness intervenes between the soul and its Maker to hinder or diminish their relation of friendship and love. This is that peace which the Word became Incarnate to give to men of good-will, which He bestowed upon His Apostles, and through them on us, who are one with them in 'doctrine and fellowship.' It is that peace which the world knows not, which it cannot give, and which it is as powerless to take away.

We too have our suffering and our sorrow, some in one way, and some in another. 'The heart knoweth its own bitterness.' Suffering is the heritage of the fallen race, entailed upon it by the transgression of its head and parent. But besides this it is the necessary lot of the Christian. Our Christianity is not a guarantee to us against suffering; nay, in virtue of it, by our very profession of it, we accept and expect and court it. He suffered, and so must we, if we are to be like Him, and if we are one with Him—one in the oneness of the moral unity and supernatural life of the Mystical Body. What He did once, He doeth ever. He suffered once, in the days of His flesh; but how does He, how can He suffer now? He has passed beyond the reach of death; death hath no more dominion over Him; and so He is beyond the reach also of suffering and of sorrow. He has entered upon the life invisible and immortal; and it would require a new miracle for Him to be able again to suffer and die. Even on the altar where He exists in an estate of mystical suffering and death, immolated as the Divine victim, there is no real suffering and no real death. It is not a new and oft-repeated death; it is a continuation and extension beyond the boundaries and limits of time and place of the one Passion and Death undergone on Calvary eighteen centuries ago.

Does He, then, really suffer now? He does. He suffers in us, the members of His mystical Body; and we, as says St. Paul, 'fill up in our flesh those things that are wanting of the sufferings of Christ.'

Christians—we are taken up into His unity; our lives into the oneness of His life; and therefore also our sufferings into the oneness of His. He identified His suffering, persecuted members with Himself, when He said to Saul, 'Saul, Saul, why persecutest thou Me?'

It was by reason of their realisation of this truth that the Apostles were not only steadfast under persecution, but rejoiced in tribulation, and counted it honour and joy to suffer in Him, with Him, and for Him.

In then our hours of greatest suffering, whether of mental anguish or of physical agony,—even when the whole lower nature is wrenched and torn and convulsed and quivering, and breaks out into the words, 'Father, if it be possible, let this chalice pass from me'—even then, if by the aid of Divine grace we can but add those other words, 'Nevertheless, not my will, but Thine be done,' then even of that our hour of sorrow we can say with our Mother, the Mother of Sorrows, '*Exultavit spiritus meus,*'—'My spirit hath rejoiced.'

III.

In Deo Salutari meo.
In God my Saviour. *St. Luke* i. 47.

WHEN the will of Adam rebelled against the Will of God, the entire human race was placed by his rebellious act in a state of damnation. From that moment it needed a Saviour; and God alone, Who created it, could redeem it.

According to the original Divine idea, man was to be immortal and impassible, to live for ever, and to know no suffering, either of mind or body; he was, moreover, by means of an infused gift of knowledge, and in virtue of the as yet unclouded light of his reason, to be free from the defect of ignorance and the infirmity of error.

This ideal, eternally existing in the mind of God, was realised in the first man and the first woman at their creation, during their innocence, and until their fall.

But those gifts of immortality, impassibility, felicity, and knowledge were not all, and they were not their greatest gifts. They were preternatural gifts; but they were not supernatural.

They were *preternatural,* for there was no necessity why they should be bestowed upon man in order that he should be man. He would have been equally man without them then, as he is equally man without them now. They were, then, preternatural, or beyond nature, inasmuch as they were not demanded by any exigence of his nature. They were not required in order to the existence of that nature, as such.

But they were not supernatural, inasmuch as they did not raise him to a higher order than the human, and did not bestow upon him superhuman qualities, capacities, and rights.

Now besides bestowing upon man those preternatural gifts which developed his nature to its highest conditions as such, his Creator constituted him in a state of sanctifying grace. And this was a *supernatural* gift. This raised him to an order above the human, nay! above the higher than human, the angelic—as such, that is, with the merely natural perfections of angels, — it made him *consortem Divinæ naturæ,*—a 'partaker of the Divine nature,' and an adoptive son of God; and gave him qualities, capacities, and rights which did not belong to him simply as man.

In the first place it gave him *qualities*. It gave his soul a supernatural beauty and brilliance, and lustre and radiance, and lovableness and attractiveness which, simply as a soul, it would not have possessed. And, in virtue of those qualities, that soul was to its Maker not merely an object of pleasure and complacency and satisfaction in the beholding of it, but it was an object of His necessary love. His *necessary* love, I say, for God would not have been God if He had not loved that soul which He had Himself made intrinsically lovable. He was not merely attracted or impelled to love it, but He was, so to speak, compelled by a law of His own being—by an exigence of His own spiritual life, in virtue of that perfection whereby He necessarily loves the lovable—to love that soul.

Moreover, the natural issue of this necessary love was a desire on the part of God to enter into and take possession of, to dwell and reign within that soul. And this the Triune God did in the self-same instant in which He constituted it in a state of sanctifying grace.

But, again, this gift of sanctifying grace not only endowed the soul of man with supernatural qualities, it gave it also supernatural *capacities*—whereby it could perform acts which, apart from those capacities, and in virtue of its merely natu-

E

ral or even of its preternatural powers and forces and faculties, it was absolutely incapable of. It could elicit acts of the supernatural, theological virtues of faith and hope and charity; and its acts also of the natural and moral virtues of justice and prudence, of temperance and fortitude, were, in virtue of this sanctifying grace, clothed with a supernatural character and value.

Finally, the gift of sanctifying grace invested the soul of man with supernatural *rights*; and those threefold—1. With a right to actual graces in all time of need, that is to say, whenever he willed to perform a supernatural act, such as to resist a temptation or to accept and bear a cross. 2. If he corresponded with and used those actual graces, he thereby merited a proportionate increase of his habitual sanctifying grace, with all its qualities and capacities. And 3. he merited a correlative and proportionate increase of glory in the future. His future was in his own hands, his eternal destiny was at his own disposal. Once constituted in sanctifying grace, he could determine it as he willed. If he reached the end of his probation in a state of grace, he would enter on the estate of glory; and according to the measure and character of his grace in time, so would be the measure and character of his glory to all eternity.

Such was the eternal Divine idea, intention, and design with regard to man, and it was realised in Adam.

Adam was constituted, moreover, in this supernatural estate, not merely as an individual, as an unit of the human race, and for his own personal benefit; but as the parent and head of the whole race, and for the benefit of his entire posterity. The whole human race that was to spring from him then existed in him, and with his estate its estate was identified.

If Adam passed unscathed through his period of probation and his time of trial, he would himself be confirmed in grace and translated to its correlative estate of glory; and he would also, as head and parent of the human race, transmit to all his posterity, along with their humanity, that selfsame supernatural gift of sanctifying grace which he himself possessed. If, on the contrary, he fell beneath that temptation, even should he himself as an individual rise again from his fall, yet every child of his would be conceived and born, deprived and destitute of that sanctifying grace. It was given not merely to the human person, the first man, but to the human nature then in its entirety subsisting in that person; and upon the act of that person its continuance or its loss depended.

Now, on what did the continued possession or the loss of this supernatural gift of sanctifying grace to himself and to his posterity, to the human race in him, depend? It depended on the union of his will with the will of his Maker.

To test the stability of his will, his Maker gave him a precept which was a manifestation of His will. He gave him a commandment about an, in itself, indifferent matter, but which had its obligation and its value, inasmuch as it was an external expression of the will of God. Moreover, He permitted him to be subjected to a temptation, not indeed alone, unaided and unarmed, but sustained, supported, and strengthened by a grace.

The free will of Adam stood midway between the temptation and the grace, each of which, the one on the one side, and the other on the other, attracted, allured, and influenced him, but neither of which laid on his will a shadow of compulsion, necessity, or constraint.

That Adam yielded to the temptation, that he severed his will from its union with the will of his Maker, you know. But what were the consequences of that severance?

The one great consequence was the loss of sanctifying grace, with all which that loss implied and entailed.

With it he lost also all the preternatural gifts of which I have spoken. Their possession depended upon his continued possession of it; and their loss was consequent upon its loss. But the loss of them was as nothing in comparison to the loss of it. Death and suffering and ignorance were evils, but evils that could consist with the possession of sanctifying grace in the present, and with the hope of glory in the future — evils, moreover, which should cease to exist when time should be no more. But if sanctifying grace were lost, all was lost, so far as heaven and the eternal glory and the Beatific Vision were concerned.

The loss of this grace placed man in a state of damnation; it deprived him of his supernatural qualities, capacities, and rights. It deprived him, in the first place, of his supernatural *qualities*; for, in the instant in which his will rebelled against the will of his Maker, in that instant his soul no longer shone with its former supernatural beauty and brilliance and lustre and radiance; it had no longer its supernatural intrinsic quality of lovableness and attractiveness; and God not only no longer desired to dwell within it, but His continued indwelling had become a Divine impossibility. He was not merely impelled, but compelled, to leave that soul. By an act of its will,

He was expelled and driven out. Moreover, it was now, in its estate of sin or deprivation of grace, become the necessary object of the Divine hatred. God was not merely tempted and inclined, or impelled, but compelled, to hate as well as to leave that sin-stained soul.

Secondly, it lost its supernatural *capacities*; it could now no longer perform any act of the supernatural life. And why? Simply because it was dead. Its former grace was its principle of life. Grace is the *anima animæ*—'the soul of the soul;' and when that was gone, it was deprived of life, and so was incapable of action. It was impotent, not merely with the impotence of a child, but impotent with the impotence of a corpse.

And, finally, it lost its supernatural *rights*—its power of meriting. It could no longer merit either increase of present grace or right to future glory. It had ceased to be a son, and so ceased to have any right to the inheritance of sons; to have any title or claim to the patrimony of the children of God.

Such was *privatively* the estate of damnation to which Adam reduced himself and his race by one act of his will—an act of rebellion against his Maker.

But this implied yet more. There were *posi-*

tive consequences. An offence had been committed, and for that offence the Divine justice demanded punishment, vengeance, and satisfaction. A defeat had been sustained, and the vanquished lay in an estate of captivity and bondage to his conqueror.

No man can serve two masters, but every man must serve one. By an exigence of his being, by a law of his existence, he must be in subjection and do service to some one—to his Father in Heaven or to his foe in hell, to God or to the devil. Whoso obeyeth the law of God is the servant of God, the friend of God, and the son of God, and he is free with the freedom of the sons of God. Whoso, on the other hand, obeyeth the law of sin, becomes thereby a servant of sin, and of its author the devil, and of its punishment and consequences, of death, of hell, and the grave.

Such, then, was the destiny to which man, by his fall, reduced himself—to the estate of present death, physical and spiritual, and of future burial: burial of his physically lifeless—of his dead—body in the grave, and of his spiritually lifeless—of his dead—soul in hell.

From that moment man needed a Saviour, and that Saviour could be none other than the God Who had created him. The necessity of a 'God the Saviour' is apparent under whatever aspect we regard the fall of man.

1. As it was an *offence*. It was an infinite offence, and, as such, demanded an infinite punishment, or, in its place, an infinite satisfaction; and no one could offer an infinite satisfaction, save an infinite Saviour.

But how was the offence infinite? It was perpetrated in time, and its perpetration took but a few moments—nay, but a single moment, if we consider the aversion of the will from God, which was the formal essence of the act of rebellion. Yes, but it was committed against an infinite God; and from the dignity of the person offended the offence itself may take its character and value. If, for instance, I strike two persons, and one of those two happens to be a king, while the other is but a common person, the two assaults, although materially the same, are formally different, and deserve a different punishment. A short imprisonment or a fine might satisfy, in the one case, the demands of civil justice; whereas, in the other case, the offence would be treason, and its punishment would be death. The finite sin of man had its character of infinitude from its being an offence committed against the infinite God; and for this infinite offence there must be an infinite punishment, or, in its place, an infinite satisfaction. True that, absolutely, God could have simply condoned the offence without any satisfaction at all; or He might have decreed to accept a finite satisfaction offered to Him by some holy but mere creature. But in neither case would the rigorous requirements of the Divine Justice have been satisfied; and so, to satisfy these adequately and entirely, there was to be, and was, a 'God the Saviour.'

Again, man had lost his life, both of soul and body. As to his natural life—the life of the body—he was no longer immortal. His body was a body of death. It was gravitating towards death by its own weight. The principle of death—the seeds of death—were within him. Now, in the present, he lay under sentence of death—he lived within the shadow of death—and in the future was the absolute certainty of death itself. But, as to his soul, its death was already accomplished. That death was instantaneous and complete. His supernatural life—the life of his soul—was gone. He was spiritually dead in trespasses and sins.

Now, as in the natural order man can neither acquire life for himself nor bestow it upon others, and this is true of all forms of life, the lowest as well as the highest—the organic, whether vegetative or sensitive, as well as the intellective—so also in the supernatural order, and *a fortiori*, man is incapable of regaining spiritual life for himself, or of bestowing it upon, or of transmitting it to others. Life, in all its forms, natural and supernatural, belongs inalienably to the Living God, Whose name is the Lord of Life, and in Whose Hands are the issues of life and death. Hence our Divine Lord said, '*Ego sum Vita*'—' I am the Life;' and declared at Capharnaum that He was come ' to give life unto the world,' that men might have life, and that they might have it more abundantly.

What I have said as to restoration of the lost spiritual life applies also to the acts which are its issue and result; which flow from and manifest that life. Just as the concurrence and co-operation of the Creator is required for all our acts in the natural order, whether of the organic or of the intellectual life, so also is His grace or supernatural concurrence and coöperation necessary for all our acts in the supernatural order.

Finally, a Saviour, and a Divine Saviour, a ' God the Saviour,' was necessary in order to the restitution of the *rights* which man had lost. Deprived of habitual sanctifying grace, men had no right to actual graces—no principle of meriting, and no claim or title to, the eternal glory, the heritage of sons, and the patrimony of the children of God. All their rights depended upon their sonship; on their generation from the first Adam; on their being his posterity; on their being consubstantial with him; of the same nature as his. He had grace as their parent and head; and had he persevered in grace, and been confirmed in grace, that grace would have descended from him to men along with their humanity. They would have been, one and all, conceived immaculate, and born in a state of sanctifying grace.

Do not mistake me, and suppose that injustice has been done to the human race by the Divine permission of the sin of Adam. We sinned in him, we fell in him. But might we not have sinned and fallen also ourselves? Had he persevered in his original innocence, we should have indeed been born in grace, as he was created in grace; but although constituted in grace, he was not confirmed in grace, and so neither should we have been. We should individually have had our period of probation, and our time of trial, even as he had; and if he fell before the tempter, do you suppose that you and I should have withstood and overcome?

Such, then, were the consequences of the fall of Adam to himself and to his race, and such the necessities for a 'God the Saviour,' Who should be a Mediator of God and men, and have an office in respect of both. In regard to God, He must propitiate and satisfy for the offence committed. In regard to men, He must be clothed with a paternity and headship, and merit to be a fountain and source and wellspring of grace to His posterity.

Hence the Divine idea of the salvation and restoration of the fallen race. A new race was to be constructed and built up from out the ruins of the old; a new family to be begotten; men were to be born again, to put off the old Adam, and to put on the New; to dissolve their moral connection with the first man, who was of the 'earth, earthy,' and to enter into a moral connection and real union with 'the Second Man, Who is the Lord from Heaven.' Thus they should have power to become the 'sons of God,' being made 'partakers of the Divine nature;' and thereby they would regain their supernatural qualities, capacities, and rights.

Hence the prophecies concerning 'God the Saviour,' the Mediator of God and men, that He was to have the heathen 'for His inheritance, and the kingdoms of the earth for His possession;' that He was to be ' *Pater futuri sæculi*,'—' the Father of the future age;' that He was to 'see His seed, and to be satisfied,'—a great multitude that no man could number, gathered out of every kingdom and nation and people and tongue, which He had redeemed to Himself by His Blood.

We should have an entirely inadequate notion, a miserable misconception, a meagre and dwarfed idea of the work of God our Saviour, if we confined our idea of the mediatorial work of the Incarnate Word to what He did upon the Cross of Calvary, or even during the years of His mortal sojourn on earth and among men. Our conception, to be adequate and true, must include what He did by His Ascension into Heaven, and what He is doing now. All are parts of one consistent Divine scheme; and the disruption or dislocation and severance of those parts the one from the other is that which has given rise to not a few of the myriad forms of error and misbelief which obtain outside the Catholic Church with regard to the manner of the existence of that Church, its constitution and scope, the laws of its life, and the modes of its operation.

The sacrifice of the Cross was a perfect and adequate, because an infinite propitiation and satisfaction to the offended God for all the sins of the entire race; but it had to be applied, in its efficacy, individually to each member of the human race. It was the sacrifice of the Father for His children, of the Head for the members of His Body; and in the fruits of that sacrifice, those members and those children have their share. Observe, I do not say that He died only for the predestinate, or that He died only for the faithful. He gave Himself a sacrifice for all—for Jew and Gentile, for Heathen and Christian, for Turk and Protestant and Infidel; there was no exclusion. The redemption was as universal as the mediation, and that was between God on the one hand and the entire fallen race on the other. And the redemption included also Mary.

Yet, how might this be? Was not Mary sinless? Is it not true that on her immaculate soul there never lay the slightest stain of the original transgression?—that that peerless soul was ever radiant with the lustre and beauty of Divine grace?—that the words of Gabriel in after years, '*Ave, gratia plena!*' might have been said to her, and would have applied to her in the first instant of her human life?

Yes, undoubtedly this is true; and yet, as undoubtedly, it is also true that she was a descendant of the fallen Adam, in whom, as in their head and common father, the human race sinned and fell and died the death of the soul. She was a daughter of Eve, the first human sinner, and the universal mother of all the spiritually dead, as well as of all the naturally living.

As such, then, she ought, as it were, by rights, to have been conceived with the stain of original sin upon her soul; and this she would have been save for a singular privilege bestowed upon her by her Maker, and that in view and in virtue of the future prospective merits of Him Who, from her flesh and blood, was to derive His own.

Hence it is that Mary was redeemed, and that her Divine Son was her Redeemer. Hence it is that she calls Him in a special manner *her* Saviour: 'My spirit hath rejoiced in God *my* Saviour.' He was *her* Saviour in a manner special to herself. He came, suffered, and died, '*propter nos homines et propter nostram salutem*,'—'for us men and for our salvation;' but He came more for Mary and for her redemption than for all the world beside. It cost Him more to purchase her Immaculate Conception than to purchase the new births unto grace of a world, every individual of which was conceived in iniquity, and, with one or two singular exceptions, such as Jeremias and St. John the Baptist, brought forth in sin. Hence it is that to her the Church applies the words of the Heavenly

Bridegroom in the canticle, *Vulnerasti Cor Meum, amica Mea, sponsa Mea!*' 'Thou hast wounded My Heart, My sister, My spouse!'

This is what the Roman Pontiff, the Vicar of Christ, our **Holy Father, Pius IX.**, now happily reigning, **specially** points out and **lays** peculiar stress on, when, in his Dogmatic Bull declaring his definition of the Immaculate Conception of Mary as a revealed truth to be believed in by every Christian who would not make **shipwreck** of the faith, he teaches, **that Mary, in the first** instant of her conception, **by a** singular **grace** and privilege of Almighty **God, and** in view of **the merits of** Jesus Christ, the Saviour of the human race, was preserved free from all stain of original sin.

And as it was with her Immaculate Conception, so was it also with every grace of the entire series of graces which together made up the sum of her spiritual life while she was yet *viatrix*,—in the estate of the **way,** and with the power of meriting and receiving 'grace for grace.' For this grace of the Immaculate Conception, magnificent as it was, was only her first; **it was only** the foundation-stone of the edifice of her spiritual life. 'Her foundations,' says the Church, applying to her the words of the Psalmist her progenitor, 'were upon the holy hills.' And again of her Isaias says: 'In the last days the mountain of the House of the Lord shall be prepared on the top of mountains, and it shall be exalted above the hills.' The mountains and hills of which the prophet and the psalmist speak are the angels and the saints of God; and their meaning is, that Mary began where those holy ones ended; that her grace, in the first moment of her human life far exceeded the sum of their united graces, accumulated by years of struggle and conflict, of labour and toil.

If such was Mary in the first instant in which she was capable of holiness, what must she have been at the date of the Annunciation, when nearly sixteen years had passed away, and those years had been one continuous series of uninterrupted acts of faith and hope and charity, each meritorious of a fresh grace in the present, as well as of a corresponding eternal 'weight of glory' in the future? Not a single affection, emotion, thought, wish, or desire had ever for a moment tended towards the creature, fastened on it, and rested in it, as if that creature were her end. All had been ordained and directed towards her Last End, the God in Whom she lived and moved and had her being. Throughout those years, God,—the Triune God, the Father, the Son, and the Holy Ghost,—had been dwelling within her, reigning over her with undisputed

sway, possessing her absolutely, and rejoicing in
that possession day by day more and more, as day
by day she became by the operation of His grace
more valuable, more beautiful, more lovely and
more desirable.

Innocent as the first Eve when she came from
the hand of God, Mary possessed that integrity of
nature which was the preternatural prerogative of
unfallen innocence. In virtue of that integrity,
there were in her no irregular inclinations, no way-
ward desires, no inordinate affections, no temptations from within ; for in her was no *fomes peccati*,
no root of sin, no law in her members warring
against the law in her mind, and striving to bring
it into captivity to the law of sin and death.
There was ever in her the most perfect subjection
of body to soul, of the lower nature to the reason,
of the reason to the will, and of the will to God ;
and thus the soul of Mary was in a perfect state of
ever-increasing and ever-intensifying union with
its Maker.

Now, of all this accumulation of merits, of all
this wealth of holiness, He, who was to be her
very own child, flesh of her flesh, blood of her
blood, was the author and the meritorious cause.
Her graces were antecedent effects, anticipated
results of His Cross and Passion, which as yet lay

distant in the future by a space of more than thirty years. Just as to the Jews the Passion was as if it were already past—just as the contrition of the first Adam and the first Eve, and the tears of David, were purchased by the Bloodshedding and Death of the Second Adam, who was to be the Son of David—so to Mary, the Second Eve, and the queenliest daughter of that royal house, the Cross and Passion of her unborn, nay, of her as yet unconceived child, was as if it were already past; and all that she had and all that she was, she owed to Him as her Redeemer.

Let us fix our thoughts for a moment on that last grace which she received previous to the descent and overshadowing of the Holy Ghost, the Hypostatic Love of the Father and of the Son, her Divine Spouse; that grace the last of the series which made up her first sanctification, the sanctification which was the preparation for her maternity; that grace wherewith the Most High completed His sanctification of 'His own Tabernacle'—'*Sanctificavit Tabernaculum Suum Altissimus*'—and which completion drew the Eternal Word from the Bosom of the Eternal Father, and caused Him to take up His created residence within her, by the force of that attractiveness which He Himself had bestowed upon her.

Mary knelt, in the solitude and silence of the night on the 25th of March within her humble chamber,—the inner room of a lowly cottage, in an obscure hamlet among the hills. She was wrapt in an ecstasy of Divine contemplation,—she was lost in God. Before her mind lay outspread, like a vast panorama, the whole of her magnificent God-given knowledge.

On the one hand, lay her knowledge of the Divine Nature, Perfections, and Attributes, of the Threefold Personality, the Paternity of the Father, the Filiation of the Only-begotten, the Procession from Both as from one principle and by one spiration of the term of Their mutual love, the Third Divine Person, God the Holy Ghost.

On the other hand, lay outspread her knowledge of the Divine external operations in the universe of creatures — the creation of the angels, their sanctification and trial, the fall of Lucifer and the victory of Michael,—the creation, sanctification, temptation, and fall of the human race in Adam,—the infinitude of that sin, and the necessity for an infinite reparation, redemption, and satisfaction, — the promise of the Woman and the Woman's Seed, of the Second Adam and the Second Eve, of the Incarnate Word, and of the Mother of God.

During the years of her seclusion in the temple cloister, preceding her betrothal to him whom God had chosen and given her for her virgin consort, Mary had pondered the prophecies concerning those two, and the types of both contained in the Hebrew Scriptures. Those meditations had produced in her mind a vivid image of the future Mother and her Divine Child; of the Virgin who was to conceive and bear Emmanuel—God with man; of the Child on whose shoulder should be laid the government, and whose name should be called Wonderful, Counsellor, the Strong God, the Father of the future age, and the Prince of Peace.

The realisation of that image, and, if it might be, to behold it with her own eyes, was the continual subject of her desires and prayers. Like the aged Simeon and the holy Anna, she longed that her eyes might see her Saviour, the Light who was to lighten the Gentiles as well as to be the Glory of His own people Israel.

That that blessed among women should be a daughter of Eve, of the seed of Abraham, of the race of Isaac, of the house of Israel, of the tribe of Judah, and of the lineage of David, she knew. Those conditions met in her own person. But that she herself should be that Virgin Mother who should be thus blessed above all women, she as yet knew not. It had not been revealed to her, and the perfection of her matchless humility prevented the very suspicion of the thought. She would have been content to be among the lowest and the least of the handmaids of that glorious Queen ; and she would have deemed it abundant recompense to have the privilege and the right to call her—Mother !

But those were not the only thoughts of the heart of Mary.

No one had ever realised, as she had, the vision of sin,—not even Michael, when, on fire with a holy anger, he drove the first sinners into the abyss. In herself Mary could have no experience of sin, but outside and around her she had seen it, till her soul was sick and weary, and turned away and found its rest again in God. Wherever she bent her steps or turned her eyes she saw sin, in itself, in its evidences, and in its effects. She could not live in a world that was lying in wickedness, and remain unconscious of the existence of sin ; and no one had ever fathomed the depths of sin as had the sinless soul of Mary, for no one had ever soared so high in contemplation of the Supreme. She apprehended its foul malignity, its atrocious ingratitude, its infinite character as committed against an Infinite God, the infinite chasm of separation which it had cleft between the Creator and His own creature—a chasm that could only be bridged across by an infinite satisfaction, offered and accepted and paid to atone for and expiate the infinite injury and offence done to Infinite Justice and Holiness.

As a consequence of this knowledge, she also knew that the promised Messias, who was to restore the human race, and to reconcile man to his Maker, would be—a victim; that the fairest among the sons of men would be shorn of His beauty and comeliness; that He would be despised and an abject, a scorn of men and an outcast of the people, a man of sorrows and acquainted with infirmity—as it were a leper, struck by God and afflicted. She knew that the Immaculate Lamb, the Lamb of God, would be led as a sheep to the slaughter; that He would tread the winepress alone; and that, among all the sorrows of a world of sorrows, there would be no sorrow like unto His sorrow. The words of her royal ancestor were familiar to her, in which the Psalmist, identifying himself with his Divine Descendant,—David, speaking in the person of the Son of David, says, 'O God, My God, look upon Me; why hast Thou forsaken Me? I am a worm, and no man, the reproach of men, and the outcast of the people. All they that saw Me have laughed Me to scorn; they have spoken with the lips and wagged the head—"He hoped in the Lord, let Him deliver Him; let Him save Him, seeing He delighteth in Him." They have opened their mouths against Me, as a lion ravening and roaring. I am poured out like water, and all My bones are scattered. My heart is become like wax, melting in the midst of My bowels. My strength is dried up like a potsherd, and My tongue hath cleaved to My jaws, and Thou hast brought Me down into the dust of death. For many dogs have encompassed Me; the council of the malignant hath besieged Me. They have dug My hands and feet. They have numbered all My bones. They have looked and stared upon Me. They parted My garments amongst them; and upon My vesture they cast lots.'

Could there be a more vivid picture of the horrors of Calvary?

David, gazing in prophetic vision through the vista of a thousand years, not only speaks of the Passion as if he were an eye-witness, but as if he were himself identified with the victim. But if such an identification in spirit was possible to an ancestor so remote, what must necessarily be the identification of one who was so near,—what must be a mother's share in the sufferings of her son?

That mother would participate in those agonies in a measure adequately corresponding to the closeness of her relation. That mother would be a mother indeed of joy and glory, but she would be a mother also of sorrows. She would be Queen of Patriarchs, of Prophets, of Apostles, and of Angels; but she would also be Queen of Martyrs. And this title, *Regina Martyrum*, would belong to her, not only as enthroned in dignity far above all martyrs, but also, and chiefly, inasmuch as the sufferings of her own martyrdom should far surpass the combined sufferings of all who have resisted unto blood striving against sin, and laid down their lives for the testimony of Jesus.

Now all this Mary certainly knew, and that by reason not only of her gift of infused knowledge bestowed upon her along with other gifts, and the habitual grace which sanctified her in the first moment of her being, but also as a consequence of her prayerful study and contemplation of the prophecies, her understanding aided and illuminated by a special assistance and light of God the Holy Ghost. Moreover, the knowledge of this was, in a manner, due to her, not only in virtue of her peerless sanctity, but also in view of her predestined office. She apprehended and realised to the full the sacrifice that Mother would be called upon to make—the maternal mental anguish necessarily accompanying and bound up with the honour and exaltation, the joy and glory of being Mother of God. These two,—her royalty in martyrdom, and the royalty of her maternity,—her motherhood of sorrow and the motherhood of God,—were as closely connected, as really related, and as dependent the one upon the other, as the two ideas of the Incarnate God and the Suffering God,—the glorified God-Man and the Man of Sorrows.

Unless we clearly apprehend this, we fail to understand the value of Mary's consent to the message of Gabriel, which proposed, in order to her coöperation, the purpose of her Maker.

For otherwise where would have been the merit of her consent; and why should the Creator thus stand, as it were, on ceremony with His own creature? To accept an honour above all honours,—a glory and a blessedness impossible to the Seraphim,—would have been simply to obey the first promptings of natural inclination and human impulse; it would have had no merit, and would have required no grace. But to consent to, voluntarily to accept, and deliberately to take upon herself such a share as hers must necessarily be, such a share in the immolation of the Divine Victim, in the sacrifice, in the sufferings, and in the shame of the

Crucified God as was possible to the creature,—
such a combination of sacrifices, of unequalled suffering, an anguish surpassing all human anguish,
an agony which, without a special supernatural
strengthening, no human being could endure and
live,—this, mere human nature would have rejected
a thousand times, and so rejecting it, would have
instinctively followed its natural inclination and
acted on its natural impulse. Not even the anticipation of eternal reward and of the future glory
would have sufficed to weigh in the balance against
the weight of that cross of present suffering which
had to be borne. It required the strength of
Divine grace, of the graces, and of all the graces
of Mary, to enable her to elicit her consent, and
to utter the words, '*Fiat mihi secundum verbum
tuum*,'—'Be it done to me according to thy
word.' The *Fiat* of Nazareth was the correlative
of, and the nearest approach to the *Fiat* of Gethsemani, when, in the extremity of the agony of Jesus,
nature asserted itself and manifested its repugnance
to suffering and shame in the 'Father, if it be
possible, let this chalice pass from Me;' and grace
triumphed in His '*Veruntamen non Mea, sed fiat
voluntas Tua*,'—'Nevertheless, not My will, but
Thine be done.'

What a supreme moment was not that which

elapsed between the last words of the Angel and the first words of Mary! The Divine purpose decreed from eternity had come close up, and was submitted to her will. Its accomplishment rested upon her decision. The glory of God and the salvation of men were in her hands. The word which was to express her consent, and procure both, it lay with her to utter. Physically and absolutely,—it was in the power of Mary to refuse. Her will was entirely free. There rested not on it a shadow of necessity, compulsion, or constraint to destroy, or mar, or lessen the value and merit and heroicity of her consent. And yet, wonderful Divine paradox! her colossal graces made the refusal of her consent a moral impossibility. God gave Mary such a grace as He foresaw she would freely consent to; and that grace was given in view and in virtue of the prospective merits of that Divine Son whose conception should be effected by her consent.

And hence in that moment when the words of Mary were uttered, and the Word of God was made flesh,—Mary rejoiced in God her Saviour.

Again, when Calvary was come, and Mary stood beneath the Cross, and shared, as she gazed on, the death agonies of her Divine Son; when the iron entered the deeper into her soul as she realised that *she* was crucifying Him, that *her* hand held the hammer and drove the nails and thrust the spear, that *she* was more His crucifier, not only than any individual of the human race, but than all the human race beside,—even then, when her soul was wrung with an almost intolerable anguish, —her spirit rejoiced in God her Saviour.

And in Him, as her Saviour, the glorified spirit of Mary is rejoicing now. She rejoices in Him, as a beatified creature rejoicing in its Divine Creator. She rejoices in Him, as a mother rejoicing in her first-born, her only-begotten and her well-beloved Son. But she rejoices also, and with a special joy, in Him—as God her Saviour.

Mary is His greatest triumph, His noblest trophy,—and we do well to remember this. It is an aid to faith. Sometimes our hearts grow sick within us as we see how little apparent results there are for so vast an outlay. Jesus shed His Blood, willing thereby that all men should be saved, and should come to the knowledge of the truth. And yet, after eighteen centuries, but a portion of the world professes Christianity, and of that portion how great a number tread underfoot the Blood of the Everlasting Covenant, and crucify the Son of God afresh, and put Him to an open shame. Even among the just what a waste of grace, and each grace precious with the preciousness of the Precious Blood! We are tempted sometimes almost to think of Christianity as if it were at best but a gigantic failure. We turn our eyes to Mary, and in her light we see light.

Were she, 'our tainted nature's solitary boast,' the one only result of the death of her Divine Son,—were the whole human race, save Mary, lost, His work on earth would not have been a failure, and He would not have died in vain. Better, so far as the interests of God are concerned,—better, so far as regards the accidental glory He derives from His human creatures—better to have Mary saved, and all save Mary lost, than to have had the human race without exception saved, and that there should have been no Mary.

'The idea of the sinlessness of Mary derogates from the Redemption of her Son;' so say men who know not Mary; and, because they know not Mary, know not Jesus. They cannot know the Mother who know not the Son; and they can never know the Son who know not the Mother. Without the twin knowledge of those twain whom God hath joined together, and whom man may not put asunder, we cannot enter into Mary's heart, and ponder with Mary the meaning of her words. '*Exultavit spiritus meus in Deo Salutari meo,*'— 'My spirit hath rejoiced in God my Saviour.'

IV.

Respexit **humilitatem ancillæ Suæ**.

He hath regarded the humility of His **handmaid**.

St. Luke i. 48.

WE come now to consider the humility of **Mary,** in virtue of which she was worthy to be Mother of God, and to be Queen of all God's creatures.

And, in the first place, what is humility? Wherein does it consist?

Humility is not self-depreciation, or a making oneself out to be less than one is, or worse than one is. It is simply the clear, conscious knowledge, the abiding and vivid recollection, the practical recognition and confession, that one is a *creature;* and, as such, has a Creator, from Whom depends, not only all that one has, but also all that one is. The virtue of humility is, in other words, the first article of the Creed—'*I believe in God*'—carried out into practice.

Now, what is it to be a creature?—and what is creation?

To be a creature is to be dependent, not only for all that one has, but for all that one is, upon another; and creation is the act on the part of that other, whereby we receive our being and our existence. Creation is not formation. It is not the transformation of a thing already existing into something else; or the bestowing upon it of greater perfections. For instance, God formed the body of the first Adam out of the clay of the earth, and gave it qualities which that clay did not possess, such as organisation, proportion, symmetry, and beauty. Now this was not creation, for there was a previous subject out of which that body was formed. But when the soul of man was, by an act of the will of the Triune God, called from nothingness into existence, then there was a pure creative act.

The definition of creation is,—the effection of a thing out of nothing—the bestowal of existence; in virtue of which that which, a moment before, was only possible, and in no way actual, becomes actual, and begins for the first time to exist and to be.

Now, to create is the inalienable prerogative of God. It belongs to Him—and to Him alone. No creature, however high, or however holy, can share or coöperate with Him in creation. No

Angel—not Mary. Nay, not the Human Soul of Jesus Christ; for there was a time when the Angels were themselves created, and when the souls of Jesus and Mary sprang from nothingness into existence. There was a particular definite moment when they, one and all, began to be, and, the moment before, they were not.

The Angels may have coöperated in the formation of the world out of its primeval state of chaos, and assisted in its disposition, ordering, and arrangement. The Angels might have assisted in the formation of the body of the first Adam, who was of the earth, earthy; and Mary did coöperate really and truly in the formation of the body of the Second Adam, who was the Lord from Heaven.

He, as man, had preternatural power over matter and over the elements. He could multiply bread—He could turn water into wine, and still the violence of the winds and waves—but He, as man, was powerless to create a human soul or to call any being from nothingness into existence. To do this belonged indeed to Him, but it belonged to Him only as He was God—as He was the Eternal Word, consubstantial and coequal with the Father and the Holy Ghost. The Triune God is the Sole Creator. He alone can create, who is Himself the

Uncreated—who has no cause—who is not even to Himself a cause—who is the self-sufficient reason of His own existence—who is the self-existent—the necessarily existing—and the fountain and source and spring and cause of existence to all outside Himself—to everything that is not God.

To create, then, belongs to God alone, and it belongs equally to the Father, to the Son, and to the Holy Ghost, inasmuch as each of those Three Persons is equally God; and, as such, possesses the self-same Divine Being, Life, Wisdom, Will, Power, and Action. They are consubstantial, coeternal, and coequal. Moreover, they are not three distinct and separate Creators, but one Creator. They create as they are *One*—for they create as they are God.

But again, creation is not a transient act, done at a given moment in the past, and ceasing. It is a continual, perpetual action, extending itself, not only from the past into the present, but from the present into the future; and enduring, not only all days, even to the consummation of the world, not only until the Latter Day, when Time shall be no more, but—throughout Eternity.

This continuation or extension of the Creative Act we call *Conservation*. It is the preservation in existence of the creature which the Creator has called, by a simple act of His will, out of no-thingness into being. **God** did not merely, at a definite moment in the past, bestow upon us existence in suchwise **as that** thenceforward we should possess that **existence** independently of Him. He continues **it to us in** every moment **by a** perpetual unceasing **inflow of** created being.

Supposing God were to decree to *annihilate* us —not merely to destroy us—not merely to deprive us of our perfections **or** qualities, as, for instance, of our life, or of our humanity, or to resolve us into our component parts or constituent elements, but—to reduce us to our original nothingness—He would proceed, **not by way of** action **or** energy, not by an **exertion of** power, not by a stroke or a blow, **but simply by a** relaxation or cessation of creative energy. **His Right Arm** would cease for a moment to sustain us—the inflow of existence from Him to us would cease **for a second—and,** in that second, we should **drop** back into that nothingness whence we sprang.

Here again you see the perpetual dependence of the creature upon its Creator. Nor is this **all.** Is our action **our own?** Can we act by ourselves independently **of our** Maker? In no **way.** Not only does the character of the action correspond **with** and follow the character of the existence,

which is its root and principle, and which existence
is dependent; but there is required a direct concurrence on the part of the Creator with every act
of the creature—with every act not only of the intellective, but also of the organic life; not only of
the sensitive, but even of the vegetative, or lowest
form of life. We cannot move hand or foot, or
draw a breath, or conceive an idea, or utter a word,
without concurrent action and direct coöperation
on the part of our Creator. In all things, and in
order to all things, we are entirely, utterly, and
absolutely dependent on the Triune God—on God
our Creator—on the Almighty who made us.

This is simply in plain words what St. Paul
taught the Athenians, standing in the midst of
their Areopagus—the doctrine which he summed
up in the words, 'God who made the world and
all things therein, ... the Lord of heaven and
earth, ... giveth to all life, and breath, and all
things . . . In Him we live, and move, and be.'

And to know this—to know that we have a
Creator, and are, as creatures, dependent upon
that Creator—requires no revelation, no supernatural gift, no light of Pentecostal faith. It is a
knowledge connatural to man, and coextensive
with the human race. It is not the heritage of
the Christian or the Jew; it is common to the

Gentiles also, who, having not the law—the Law of Moses—or the Gospel of Jesus Christ, have the Natural Law written on their hearts. By the light of nature we know that we have a Creator and that we are creatures. We know His relation, as such, towards us, and our correlative relations and consequent obligations towards Him. In evidence of this, the Apostle appeals to the utterance of the heathen poets : 'As some of your own poets have said,—For we also are His offspring.' The Psalmist, moreover, declares that it is the 'fool (who) hath said, in his heart, There is no God.' He says that the Atheist is a fool — that he is not acting as a reasoning being, that he is not using the natural light of his reason, the powers and faculties of his own nature. And farther, his denial of God is not in his intellect; it is in his heart. It is an act of a depraved and perverse will, in opposition and in contradiction to the dictates of even the unaided reason.

Humility, then, as we have defined it, is the clear, conscious knowledge, the abiding and vivid recollection, the practical recognition and confession that one is a creature, and depends absolutely and utterly for all that one has, and all that one is, upon one's Creator. It is a virtue which belongs to the natural law as well as to the Gospel; and obliges **not** the Jew only, **but** the Gentile also, **not** merely the Christian family, **but** the human race.

Again, **in** order **to be** humble, this knowledge **by the** creature **of** its dependence upon its Creator, must be—not merely speculative, but practical. **It** must **be not merely** possessed by and abiding **in** the intellect, **but** acting **on** and **moving** the will. It must be **not merely** an idea, **but an idea** carried out into action.

There **may be a** barren **and dead** faith which bears **no** fruit. There **is a** faith **of** devils who believe and **tremble; and** there **is a** faith **also of** wicked men, which may **be so** great **as to work** miracles and **to** remove mountains; and **yet, if it** have not charity, **it is as** nothing. **Those who** possess such faith practically deny by **their actions** what they may speculatively **know in their intel-** lects, and what they may even assert **with** their lips.

The fruit of humility, then, is obedience; even as the fruit of faith is charity. There is no living faith without charity; and there is no living humi- lity without obedience. As charity is the soul of faith, so is obedience the soul of humility. And this from the very nature of the case.

Our Divine Creator is not a mere power,

He is not a mere Almighty force. God is a spirit, with an intelligence and a will; and of that will He has given an external expression in a law; and by means of that law His uncreated will presses on the will of His rational creature; and when the rational creature submits beneath that pressure and obeys, it thereby confesses its created nature, and so performs an act of humility. Whereas, if, on the contrary, it opposes that will by transgressing that commandment, and breaking that law, by this its disobedience it practically denies its created nature, endeavours to be as God, and so commits a sin of pride.

We have, then, on the one hand, three virtues —humility, obedience, and charity; and we have, on the other hand, three vices—pride, disobedience, and practical infidelity. These three, on either side, go hand in hand, and are really identified. The one is the offspring or counterpart of the other; where the one is, there is the other also. Humility and pride are the two roots, foundations, mainsprings, origins, and causes of virtue and vice respectively. Humility is the foundation of obedience and charity; pride, of disobedience and practical infidelity. We ordinarily speak of obedience, of contrition, and of charity as if they were really different and distinct the one from the other; while, in truth, they are in reality one. They differ connotatively or relatively, but essentially they are identified.

What is charity save obedience? 'If ye love Me,' says our Divine Lord, 'keep My commandments.' What is contrition but the charity of one who has sinned? He has severed himself from sin, and wedded himself again to God; and this wedding or reunion of his will with the Divine Will as expressed to him by the Divine law, what is it save the very definition and idea of charity—that charity which is the end of the commandment and the fulfilling of the law and the bond of perfection?

We may take, then, humility and pride as the two distinguishing characteristics, as at once properties and notes of the two great families— the Family of the Fallen, and the Family of the Redeemed,—in like manner as they are also the two distinguishing characteristics of the heads of those families. The devil is now the head of the family of the fallen. He is the common father of the sons of pride—the children of disobedience. He was the first of creatures to say, *Non serviam,* —'I will not serve. I will be like unto the Most High.' And this is the utterance and the watchword of all who are his followers and children, or rather his captives and his bondslaves.

I say rather **his** captives **and his** bondslaves, for it is an abuse of words in any strict sense to call them children, or to speak of them **as** constituting a family. The relation between father and children **is** one which implies mutual love—which signifies **care**, protection, and solicitude on the one hand, **and,** on the other, submission, reverence, and **obedience.** The idea of **a** family implies interdependence, subordination, concord, and unity. Now, those ideas are, one and all, incompatible with the idea of the devil and of those who, by sin, are made subject unto him. They are **a** horde and not a race ; they are a legion and not a family; they are a herd and not a flock. Individual independence, insubordination, impatience of control, self-will **and** private judgment, disunion, discord, **and** disobedience, **are** their prevailing and salient characteristics—**the properties** which they possess, and the notes whereby they are known. Their sole principle and bond of unity is their hatred of God and of all that is His. '**I will put enmities**,' said God to the Archspirit of Evil, 'between thee and the Woman, between thy seed and Her Seed.'

In, on the contrary, the Family of the Redeemed we **have** the true idea of a family in its highest form—a community of nature, a community of interests and sympathies, of purposes and

desires and aims, as well as of goods or possessions.
The members of this family are of one heart and
of one mind. They have one destiny and one end.
It is a true race, derived from one Father and
one Mother; and a true family—bound together
in a family oneness with the cords of Adam—with
parental, filial, and fraternal love; and its distinguishing characteristics, its properties and qualities,
its notes and evidences, are those three—humility,
obedience, and charity.

Consider the humility of the Father of the
One Family. 'He humbled Himself,' as St. Paul
writes to the Philippians, 'and became obedient
unto death, even the death of the Cross.' This
is at first what strikes one as the greatest of the
humiliations of our Divine Lord. But it was not
the greatest. His humiliations were manifold,
and they may be reduced to five. The first was,
the Eternal Word's assuming a created nature
into the unity of His Divine Person, His clothing
Himself in the garment of our humanity, His
being found in habit as a man. The second
was, His humbling Himself through the *circumstances* of His Incarnation. Not only did He
come as the child of a poverty-stricken mother,
who found not where to lay her new-born child
save in the manger of the beasts that perish;

not only did He lead a life of hardship and privation—'The foxes have holes, and the fowls of the air have nests, but the Son of Man hath not where to lay His head;' not only did He associate Himself with the outcasts of society—with the publicans and the harlots—and provoke the derision and contempt, as well as the hatred and enmity of the self-righteous Pharisees, of the cultured Sadducees, and the courtly Herodians; not only did He select as His followers and fellow-workers the rude unlettered fishermen of Galilee; but, more than all this, He suffered that Humanity which He had assumed to be destroyed; He gave His Soul to be disembodied, His Body to be lifeless, and His Blood to be poured out upon the ground like water, and to be trodden under foot of men. And this too by a death reserved for the lowest of the people and the worst of criminals—a death upon the tree of shame, and between two malefactors.

And yet this was not all. 'It became Christ to suffer, and so to enter into His glory.' But after He had entered upon that glory; after He had conquered hell, and risen triumphant and victorious from the grave; after, earth being no longer a fit abode for Him, He had 'ascended up on high, leading captivity captive;' after He had entered on the life invisible and immortal; after His created Humanity had been exalted to the Right Hand of the Eternal Father, seated on the Great White Throne, clothed in all the splendour and brightness of the Beatific Glory, and worshipped by all the angels who stand before God; after His Sacred Body had become the central sun of the heavenly Jerusalem,—after all this, He still and again humiliates Himself, and will so humiliate Himself all days, even to the consummation of the world, shrouding not only His Divinity in the garment of His Humanity, but His glorified Humanity itself in the swaddling-clothes of the sacramental species. Again He becomes obedient unto death,—not that He really repeats His one death and dies again, but,—inasmuch as His ever-recurring mystical death upon the altar is a perpetual continuation and extension throughout time, and in every place, of His one death upon the Cross of Calvary. He, in the plenitude of His glory, in the height of His exaltation—He, living with the full tide of His heavenly life—comes and goes at the will of another, and is handled and treated as if helpless, as if deprived of all power of motion, and destitute of all means of resistance. Thus does He everlastingly confess and proclaim His possession of a created nature—reducing His Humanity, which, as now existing in heaven, exists there developed to its highest conditions, to its lowest mode of existence—to the lowest mode compatible with the existence of a living body—to a mode which trembles on the very borders of annihilation.

But, even so, we have not fathomed His condescension. There is yet a lower deep into which the Most High can descend—and that is His entrance into a sinner's soul. We read, with almost horror, the Gospel narrative of His suffering Himself to be borne through the air from the wilderness of Quarentana to the top of a high mountain in the foul grasp of the Spirit of Evil; but it is in reality a greater humiliation to enter into the foul soul of a sinner. To give Himself to Judas on the Thursday night was a greater humiliation than to lay down His life upon the first Good Friday.

Here, then, in the Father of the One Family, we have the archetypal pattern and the supreme perfection of humility. His was a created human soul; and He ever recognised and confessed its created existence by conforming and submitting its will to the will of its Creator. To do His will was, He declares, His meat and drink. 'Lo, I come to do Thy will, O My God.' 'Father, not what I will, but what Thou wilt!' 'Not My will, but Thine be done.'

And, as with the Father, so with the Mother of the great Family of the Redeemed. Listen to her words and to His. She said, 'Behold the handmaid of the Lord; be it done to me according to thy word.' And of her and of all who follow her footsteps, He declared, 'Blessed are they who hear the word of God, and keep it.'

Mary makes, indeed, the greatest impression upon us when she is presented to us clothed with her maternity; and that maternity is certainly the greatest evidence of her greatness—but it is not that wherein her greatness consists. Her greatness consisted in that whereby she was worthy to be invested with her peerless position, privileges, and prerogatives, whereby she was made worthy to become the Mother of God—it consisted in the perfection of her humility, her obedience, and her charity.

Apart from her maternity, and before it took place, before she had knowledge that it was to be, she was the first of mere creatures—the masterpiece of the Creator—the greatest of the works of God. She was so, alike in the natural and in the supernatural order,—in her natural capacities, and in her supernatural graces. She was so *passively* in the instant of her Immaculate Conception, in the first moment in which she lived with a human life;

and, in the same instant, she was so also *actively*, for her first act was an act of humility. By the unclouded light of her matchless understanding, and in virtue of her preternatural infused gift of knowledge, she knew precisely and adequately what she had, and what she was. She clearly apprehended and perfectly realised it. And what was the result? There was no self-depreciation—why should she depreciate the gifts of God? But there was also no self-complacency, no self-congratulation, no self-admiration, no vainglory, no spiritual pride. No; she knew that she was withal a creature; that all her perfections, nay, her very being was derived; that she could not call even her existence her own; that she was dependent, and a subject; that, although she was *Regina Cœli*, she was yet *Ancilla Domini*. Her perfect act of adoration of her Maker in that moment was the offspring of her humility. She practically testified to her belief in the first article of the Creed, 'I believe in God;' to the first commandment, *Soli Deo servies*,—'Thou shalt serve God alone;' and to the commandment which comprehends all others, 'Thou shalt love the Lord thy God with all thy heart, with all thy soul, with all thy strength, and with all thy mind.'

And now let us look towards the end. Let us fix our thoughts on the latter day of Time, when

the hours, and the days, and the weeks, and the
months, and the years, and the centuries—the
various gradations and measures of successive time
—shall have rolled away, and accumulated into one
past; when the day of mercy and grace is gone for
ever; when time shall be no more; when the great
assize of the human race shall have been held, and
when sentence shall have been pronounced by that
Man whom the Father hath appointed to judge
the world in equity; when the multitude of the
reprobate on the left hand, the sons of pride and
the children of disobedience, shall have heard the
terrible words which crown their despair: 'Depart, ye cursed!' and when the great family of the
just, on the right hand, the children of humility,
of obedience, and of love, shall have heard their
gracious invitation to enter into the mansions prepared for the blessed of the Father, and to sit
down at the marriage-supper of the Lamb. Then
shall the Son of Man, the Son of Mary, the Father
of the future age, the true Abraham, the Father of
the Faithful, the common Parent of the Redeemed,
of all who have been made consubstantial with
Him, not only according to the natural, but according also to the supernatural order, of all who
have been made partakers of His living and life-
giving Humanity through the *Panis Vivus*, which

is the *Panis Vitæ*—the Living Bread, which is the Bread of Life—and who have thereby been made partakers of the Divine Nature—*Consortes Divinæ Naturæ*—who have become sons of **God**, as united to, identified, and one with the Only-begotten and Well-beloved, who is in the Bosom of the Father, —of all who are heirs of **God** being coheirs with Christ and inheritors of that kingdom of heaven, which is His;—then shall He, rising from the judgment throne, preceded by the Cross, surrounded by thousands and ten thousands of attendant angels, and accompanied by the Queen on His right hand, lead the way from earth to heaven, to open its gate to all believers. 'Lift up your gates, O ye princes, and be ye lifted up, O eternal gates, and the King of Glory shall enter in,' cry the angels from without; and the angels from within respond, 'Who is this King of Glory?' The words of the royal psalmist make answer— 'The Lord who is strong and mighty, the Lord mighty in battle, the Lord of Hosts—He is the King of Glory.'

The *Rex regum*, the *Dominus dominantium*— the 'King of kings and the Lord of lords'—Who hath subdued His people unto Him, and triumphed, and caused them to triumph, over death and hell and the grave, and Who has led captivity captive, stands at last within the walls of the Heavenly Jerusalem; and the gates of the Celestial City are shut behind the last of that glittering, glorious throng of men whom no man can number, who are as the stars of heaven for multitude, and like the sand which is by the sea-shore, who have been gathered out of every kindred and nation, and people and tongue—men of every race and language under heaven. Yet now all are one—partakers of one Divine Nature, living with one Divine Life—one in heart and mind, and will and action. The Sacred Heart beats with one vibration throughout the whole mystical Body, which has been redeemed and renewed, and cleansed and glorified, by the Precious Blood of the everlasting covenant which that Heart contains; and now every member of that Body unites with the Divine Head in one act—the first act performed by the entire Body, Head and members alike—in an act of humility.

There, in the midst of the city, is the Great White Throne—the throne of the Triune God, of the Father and the Son and the Holy Ghost. The central place, between the Father and the Holy Ghost, belongs to the Son of God, and therefore to the Son of Man—the Incarnate Word. But before He seats Himself on that throne, from which He, clad in the garment of our flesh, shall reign for ever and ever—before He places His Immaculate Mother on the second throne set for the Queen, the King's Mother, at the King's right hand—before He assigns to His children and to hers, to His subjects and to hers, their several thrones, from which they shall reign with Him and her—St. Paul tells us, in that wonderful dogmatic chapter of his, the fifteenth of his First Epistle to the Corinthians, that—He shall deliver up the kingdom to God and the Father.

He humbled Himself in time by His assumption of a created nature, and, as so humbled, His words were of Himself: '*Pater major Me est*,'—'The Father is greater than I.' He humbled Himself by His permission of the destruction of that created nature in His death upon the Cross. He humbled Himself again by his Eucharistic residence on earth all days, even to the consummation of the world, in an estate of *mystical* death, and *really* in the lowest form of existence compatible with corporeal life. And now, when all struggle and conflict and warfare is at an end; when He has brought to nought all principality and power; when He has put all His enemies under His feet; when He has vanquished the last enemy, which is death, by the glorious resurrection of all whose lives that enemy has found hid with Him in God;

when, in a word, all things have been subdued unto Him, then shall He, as Head of His Church, present that Church to the Eternal Father as a glorious Church, not having spot or wrinkle, or any such thing.

Presenting that Church, one with Himself,—as His Bride by a matrimonial oneness,—one with Himself as His Body by a corporeal oneness,—one with Himself as His offspring by a family oneness,—He, as the Celestial Bridegroom, as the Divine Head, as the Heavenly Father of His human family, humbles Himself before the Creator alike of that family and of His human soul. 'Then,' says the Apostle, 'shall the Son also Himself be subject unto Him that put all things under Him, that God may be all in all.'

V.

Ecce, ex hoc beatam me dicent omnes generationes.
Behold, from henceforth all generations shall call me blessed.

St. Luke i. 48.

WHEN Mary stood by the Cross on the hill-top of Calvary, the longing of her heart, the vehement desire of her soul, was to die with Jesus. Death, and to be with Him in the Limbus of the Fathers, was to her better than life and to be separated from Him, to be alone in the world, and childless. And yet it was His will that she should live on, and be three days desolate; and being His will, it was also hers. Nature cried out, but grace triumphed. As with Him, so with her: the 'Father, if it be possible, let this Chalice pass from Me,'—nature's assertion of itself,—died away into the free loving utterance elicited by the might of Divine grace—'Nevertheless, not My will, but Thine be done.'

Again, in like manner, when the same Mary stood by the side of the risen Jesus, on the hill-top of Olivet, the longing of her heart, the vehement desire of her soul, was to follow her Divine Son. With Him, earth was heaven to her; without Him, it was a desert, a weariness, and an exile. And yet their separation was His will, and being His will, it was hers also. She wedded her will to His, and freely and lovingly consented to prolong for fifteen years her sojourn on earth and among men; and never, even in the old days of Nazareth, were the souls of Jesus and Mary in a state of such close and intimate union as during those long years of bodily separation.

But could He not have Himself remained for at least that time longer upon the earth, and gladdened by His presence His Mother's heart? and then, when the appointed years of her pilgrimage were ended, they might have gone both together, the Second Adam and the Second Eve, to the Heavenly Paradise, to receive their reward, and to take possession of the promised kingdom for themselves and for their children, the universal family of the Redeemed.

But no! it must not be. There were deep and beautiful reasons in the counsels of God why He should go and why she should remain. 'It is expedient for you that I go away, for if I go not away, the Holy Ghost will not come unto you; but if I

go, I will send Him to you,' said our Lord Himself. And again, 'If you loved Me, you would indeed be glad, because I go to the Father.' He declares the expediency of His departure, both for
their sakes and for His own.

Although through His Ascension there accrued
to Him no increase of essential glory or joy, yet He
did therefrom derive an accidental glory; for there
was a certain becomingness that He should no
longer sojourn on the earth. During the days of
His mortal life, before His Passion, it was fitting
that He should dwell on earth, and have His con-
versation among men; but after His Resurrection,
He had entered on a life which was incorruptible
and immortal; and so the world which lies in the
shadow of death, and is subject to corruption, was
no longer for Him a meet abode. Hence He says,
'If ye loved Me, ye would indeed be glad, because
I go to the Father.'

But His Ascension was not alone for His own
glory, it was also for the advantage of men. To
Thomas He said, 'Because thou hast seen, thou
hast believed; but blessed are they who have not
seen, and yet have believed.' 'The just,' says
St. Paul, 'shall live by faith,' and 'faith is the
evidence of things that appear not.' Hitherto men
had seen and believed; they had adored a visible,

tangible object. Henceforth their adoration would take a higher flight. The eye of faith would pierce the clouds, and adore Him who is behind the veil; and so for men also it was well that He should go away, and that eyes of flesh should see Him no more.

Farther, the Ascension of Jesus contributes to the strengthening and increase of our hope. 'I go,' says He, 'to prepare a place for you; and if I go and prepare a place, I will come again, and take you to Myself, that where I am, there you may be also.' It was for Him to lead the way, and to open the gate of Heaven to all believers.

By His Ascension, He has, as it were, taken possession of Heaven in our name, and on our behalf—as the Head for all the members of His mystical Body—as a King for all His subjects who have taken His yoke upon them and brought under their wills to His obedience—as a Father for all His children, begotten to Him by the Sacrament of Regeneration, and made one with Him through the Communion of His Body and Blood. In virtue of this union, Heaven is our heritage: 'All things are yours, for ye are Christ's, and Christ is God's.'

But again, His Ascension contributes to the perfection of our charity: 'Where our treasure is, there shall our hearts be also.' 'Ye are risen with Christ,' says St. Paul; 'seek those things which are above, where Christ sitteth at the right hand of God.' But this is not all: charity is not only a turning of our wills and affections heavenwards, it is a shedding abroad of the Holy Ghost in our hearts. He, the Third Person, is the Hypostatic Charity, the Personal Love of the Father and the Son; and the most perfect operation of the Holy Ghost is charity, the diffusion of which is therefore specially appropriated to Him. 'And so,' says our Lord, 'it is expedient for you that I go away, for if I go not away, the Holy Ghost will not come to you.' And again, says the Evangelist, 'The Holy Ghost was not yet given, for that Jesus was not yet glorified.'

These considerations serve to show some of the reasons why it was expedient that He should go, and she should remain. It was well for Him, and it was well for men in general. But it was well also for her in particular, for without those fifteen years of wandering in the way of the wilderness, in the desert of this world, of exile from the heavenly country, Mary would not have been what she is at this hour; and God would have lacked a glory which those years have given Him.

The glory of the Saints redounds to the glory

of God, and the measure of their glory is commen-surate with the measure of their grace. This grace they can go on increasing and accumulating only so long as they are still upon earth,—still in the estate of the way, in which they may progress in merit,—still in the day of their mortal lives, during which they may labour and earn a reward, —and before the night cometh when no man can work. Our term of sojourn is the term of our grace.

During those fifteen years Mary continued un-interruptedly to merit fresh graces, and so ulti-mately to increase her own eternal weight of future glory; which glory was again identified with God's. During those years, moreover, her merito-rious acts of faith, of hope, and of charity acquired a new character. She now adequately walked by faith, and not by sight. During the whole period of her life, she had communed by faith with the Triune, Invisible God; but for four-and-thirty years, she had in her presence, before her eyes, in her arms, or at her side, the Visible God—the Incarnate Word. Now this was taken away, and her faith was made perfect. And so in acts of brighter and ever-brightening hope, of increased and ever-increasing, of intensified and ever-intensifying love, the days passed away into the months, and the months into the years, until the number of her allotted years was accomplished, and the Divine idea of her perfection was realised, and the sum of her graces, which should be the measure of her glory, was completed; and then, —so far as she was concerned, it was no longer necessary that she should remain,—it was expedient that she too should go away.

But there was yet another reason why it was expedient that she should remain until then. It was well for Mary herself, it was well also for the Church of God. That Church was as yet in its infancy, and needed a mother's care. The new-born Mystical Body of Christ had to be nourished with the sincere milk of the word, that it might grow thereby; and what so divinely fitting as that Mary should, by an extension of her maternal office, minister to the Mystical Body, as she had, long years ago, ministered to the Natural Body of her Divine Son. She was the strength of the Vicar of Christ during those early years of trial. The Holy Ghost had been poured out in its plenitude on the Apostolic College; but it was well that the chosen Spouse of the Holy Ghost should remain for a time in their midst in her royal and maternal character, as Queen and Mother of the sons and servants of God. She strengthened their faith, brightened their hope, inflamed their love, steadied and directed their devotion, and she herself was nourished in the way of the wilderness with the Bread of Angels—the Living Bread which cometh down from Heaven, to give life unto the world, of which, if a man eat, he shall live and not die; he shall not only have life, but he shall have it more abundantly. Day by day Mary received at the hands of the Beloved Disciple the Sacred Body of her Divine Son.

But at last the days of her pilgrimage came to an end. She had reached the brink of the waters of Jordan, and she must pass through the river to the promised land—Mary must die.

But how was this, the closing mystery of her life, to be accomplished? and why was it necessary for her? Mary was sinless. Through sin came death, and death passed upon all men, for that all have sinned. Death is the wages of sin. It could not be to pay that debt of fallen nature that Mary had to die. Death had no dominion over her. Life and immortality were the prerogatives of the estate of innocence and grace which had been hers in the first instant of her being.

And yet Mary was to die. This necessity was laid upon her by reason of her very holiness, and of that intimacy of union with her Divine Son which was its consequence. It became her to be made like unto Him—to be conformed to His Image. Like Him, she must die and remain for three days in the darkness and silence of the grave.

But how was this to be accomplished? Sinless like the first Eve in her estate of innocence, Mary had in her no seed of corruption. Disease could lay no hold upon her. Old age would come unaccompanied by aught of decrepitude and decay. There was in her no intrinsic principle of dissolution; a violent death was possible to her as it was to Him—but this was not her destiny.

And yet her death was to be a martyrdom. Mary is Queen of Martyrs, and she has two claims to the title. She endured two martyrdoms. Her first was when her Divine Son was crucified before her eyes. He suffered crucifixion in His mortal Body. She endured that crucifixion in her soul. The agonies of His soul surpassed all the tortures of His body. And the souls of Jesus and Mary were knit together in one. Her share of His torments was sufficient and more than sufficient, say the holy Doctors, to have sundered soul and body and to have caused her death. The sufferings of both victims are not to be measured by the ordinary limits of a three hours' agony, they are to be multiplied by the number of men whom there were

to redeem; and that again has to be remultiplied
by the number of the sins of each which there were
to expiate. Mary would have died **on** the hill-top
of Calvary, as He would have died in the garden
of Gethsemani before His time, without supernatural aid. She received a special strengthening
aid of Divine grace enabling her to endure her
martyrdom and live. The Almighty Father pro-
longed her life, not **by** abating her pains, but by
increasing her fortitude.

In her first martyrdom Mary **was** like John
in his caldron of boiling **oil**; she was **a** martyr as
to sufficiency of cause, although not as **to effect, by**
the laying down of life. But in her second martyrdom she was a martyr as to both. It slew her.
It was a martyrdom of love. And this is not
a figure of speech. It is a simple fact. Mary
died of Divine Love. For what is love? **It is**
a tending of the soul towards, until it finds rest
in, the object loved. Now, in the first instant **of**
her human being, in the first moment in which
she lived with a human life, all her powers had
tended towards God, and she had loved Him
with a most **perfect love.** This love had increased
and intensified with **every** moment **of her** life.
Every act of her **whole** life was supernatural, and

merited, not only an exceeding and eternal weight of glory corresponding to it in the future, but also an equal measure of fresh grace in the present. Human calculation is 'paralysed—is powerless to reckon up the sum of the graces of Mary at the date of the Incarnation, and so to measure the intensity of the first act of her love of the Incarnate Word. But that act has to be multiplied and remultiplied over and over again in a proportion equal to the acts of love elicited by her during the whole term of her intercourse with her Divine Son—in the stable cave, in the house of Nazareth, by the banks of the Nile, on the hill-top of Calvary, and during the forty days of the Risen Life. And now, what is the state of the case as she stands by His side on the summit of Olivet? Her soul is on fire with Divine love—with her maternal love of her Divine Son—added to her perfect creature's love of the Incarnate Word, as her Lord, as her Saviour, nay, also as her Creator. Her soul is straining its utmost to escape from its fleshly tabernacle—to burst the bars of its mortal prison-house,—to fly away on the wings of love with the object of its affections. It would have been simply impossible for her to remain in the body, as she beheld the treasure of her heart ascending through the air, and disappearing behind the clouds from before her eyes, had not grace come to the rescue;—and again, not by a diminution of her love, but by an access of supernatural strength to love on and live.

At last the day dawned when it was no longer necessary for her, for the Church of God, and for God Himself, that she should remain apart from the Son of her love — no longer necessary for the completeness of her own perfection, for the Church's welfare, or for the Divine Glory. It was now expedient for all that she should depart; and so God withdrew that conserving force which had hitherto kept body and soul in one, and her soul fled away on the wings of love into its eternal resting-place in the bosom of her Divine Son.

Conceive for a moment the transports of joy in heaven when Mary entered into the unveiled presence of her Maker, and beheld once more the face of her own child. Conceive the welcome of the Eternal Father to the soul of His first-born daughter — the Holy Ghost brooding over the soul of His chosen spouse — the Incarnate Word crowning the soul of His Immaculate Mother—the angels and the saints, the spirits of the just made perfect, worshipping the soul of their glorious Queen—and Joseph entering anew into the joys of his stainless marriage-bond.

And here on earth, — was there joy or was there sorrow? There were both. It was a tribulation,—but a tribulation in which they rejoiced. Still the Apostles had somewhat of Mary on the earth. Her fragrant body was in their midst. They buried her to conform her to the likeness of her Son, and returned to Jerusalem rejoicing with her in her joy.

All the Apostles who were then alive, says the ancient tradition, were present at the death and burial of their Queen, save one, and that one was Thomas. It was the same Thomas who was absent when our risen Lord appeared to His Apostles in the upper chamber late in the evening of the first Easter-day. Returning on the third day, Thomas, not unbelievingly, but true to his old instincts—it was the manner and habit of the man —desired to see for himself and to touch the sacred body of Mary. They opened the sepulchre to satisfy his devotion, but they found it empty. The grave-clothes were folded together, and spotless lilies were blooming in the place where Our Lady lay. The Lord, who fifteen years before had arisen into His resting-place, had raised thither the Ark which He had sanctified.

And now as to the fittingness of the Assumption of Mary.

There were deep and beautiful reasons why it should be so, and among them these:—first, it was for the glory of her Divine Son. She was one with the Sacred Humanity not only by a spiritual, but by a corporeal, physical oneness. The Second Adam could, with a literal exactness, apply to that Mother of Life from whose veins He had derived His Body the words which the first Adam addressed to the woman whom God had formed from out his side and given him for a helpmate: 'Thou art bone of my bone, and flesh of my flesh.' 'Caro Christi, caro Mariæ,' says St. Augustine—'The Flesh of Christ is the flesh of Mary.' And again: 'That Mary should see corruption, to conceive it, I cannot; to say it, I shudder.' It appertained to the perfection of the glory of the ascended Christ that the body of His Immaculate Mother should be assumed into heaven, and enthroned there in its own place, above the Seraphim.

But, farther, it was a fulfilment of His own promise. He Himself said to Andrew and Philip: 'Where I am, there shall also My minister be.' She had ministered to Him, not only as did the angel who strengthened Him in His agony, not only as did the holy women who ministered to Him of their substance — she had ministered to

Him of her flesh and of her blood; and in her flesh it became her to receive her reward.

Once more, it was an honour due to the Mother from the Son; and it was prefigured in Solomon, the Old Testament type of the Incarnate Wisdom. When Bethsabee, the widow of David, entered into the presence chamber of Solomon, her son, the king arose to meet her, and bowed himself before her, and sat down upon his throne, and commanded a second throne to be set for the queen, the king's mother, and she sat on his right hand, and made her petition, and the king said to her: 'My mother ask, for I must not turn away thy face.' Now, when the disembodied soul of Mary entered into the presence chamber of her Son, she made a petition, and her petition was this :—it was the assumption of her body.

Amongst other petitions of the saints, they pray for the resurrection and assumption of their bodies—in a word, for their final perfection. As separated, disembodied souls, they are in a state of imperfection. The fulness of perfection requires the reunion of soul and body, which will be accomplished in the resurrection ; and for this they long. Moreover, this longing and desire and prayer is not only in order to the completion of their own accidental beatitude, but also for the glory of God, inasmuch as He will then have from them the perfect worship of perfect human beings. This desire, common to all the saints, must have also been the desire of the glorified soul of Mary, and why should it be denied? There was no reason why it should be denied. There was but one why it should be delayed. One thing alone prevented the immediate satisfaction by the Son of His mother's prayer. It was expedient that by three days' burial she should be the more perfectly conformed to His likeness. When that was accomplished, her petition was granted. Her beatified soul returned, as did His, on the third day to the sepulchre. She assumed, once more, the garment of her flesh, and clad, like Him, in the raiment of the body, she ascended through the air and entered heaven, and was set down at the right hand of the Majesty on high. The vision of God was realised; His eternal idea of the heavenly Paradise —of a perfect woman and a perfect man.

Mary was accompanied in her glorious assumption by the angels of God, who were her subjects, as by a guard of honour rejoicing in the triumph of their human queen. But be not misled by erroneous though well-meaning pictures. Her body was not carried by the angels as if it had been a beautiful but inanimate relic. She ascended herself, in virtue of that power which belongs to all risen and glorified bodies, a property and a gift, whereby the body is so thoroughly and entirely subject to the dominion of the soul, that where the soul wills to be, there the body instantaneously is. When Elias was caught up into heaven, it was by means of a chariot and horses of fire, and not by his own power, for his was not a risen body. But Mary's was. The Church, indeed, speaks of her ascension as an assumption, but for this reason: it is to denote the distinction between it and the ascension of her Son. She ascended by her own power, but it was a power not connatural to, but bestowed upon her; while His power of ascension was connatural to Himself, and belonged to His own Divine Person. By His ascension and by her assumption the Divine Idea was realised — the Second Adam and the Second Eve, the Only-begotten Incarnate Son and God's eldest daughter; Our Father and Our Mother who are in heaven.

We are their children; we have put off the old Adam, and put on the New. Children of the first Eve, we were born in sin, and lay in darkness and the shadow of death. Children of Mary, we are born again unto grace, and have been made partakers of light and life. With Them we must suffer, if with Them we will reign. It became

Them to suffer, and so to enter into Their glory. With Them also we must die, die not only one day the death of the body, but die now unto sin, that we may live unto justice. Let us, then, live and die, believing in Jesus and Mary, hoping in Jesus and Mary, loving Jesus and Mary with our whole hearts. Both are in heaven, body and soul. They are our chiefest and our choicest human treasures; and where our treasure is, there let our hearts be also.

VI.

Vulnerasti Cor Meum, amica Mea, sponsa Mea.
Thou hast wounded My Heart, My sister, My spouse.

Cant. iv. 9.

THERE is no devotion among the many that abound in the Church of Christ, which at once gives greater glory to God, and is of greater value to the souls of men, than the devotion to the Sacred Heart of Jesus. Devotions to the Sacred Humanity include all others, but the devotion to the Sacred Heart includes all the devotions to the Sacred Humanity. Let us fix our thoughts on this devotion, and consider;—what we worship—why we worship It—what the Sacred Heart is in Itself,—and what It is in Its relations to us.

The Sacred Heart is not a mere symbol, nor is it an abstract idea; it is not the creation of our own imagination, nor is it a memory of the past. It is a physical reality—a created thing, which really existed in the past, and which as really exists now. What we worship is, not merely the love of Jesus as symbolised and represented by the Sacred Heart, but the Heart itself which throbbed and throbs with that love.

But if It be a finite created thing, why do we worship it? or why, at any rate, do we render to It that supreme absolute Divine worship reserved and due to the Infinite and Uncreated alone? Is it not idolatry to give to the creature that which belongs of inalienable right to the Creator? Most assuredly it is. Not to Mary herself, Queen of angels and of men, may we, for instance, offer sacrifice—sacrifice being the highest form of that worship which is due to the Uncreated Creator, and to Him alone.

And yet we give Divine worship to the Sacred Heart of Jesus. And to give It less, would be to give It less than is Its due. The reason is this: although It is a finite created thing, as being an essential part of a finite and created human nature, yet that nature with all its parts subsists in, is possessed by, and belongs to no human person. It subsists in, is possessed by, and belongs to a Divine Person,—the Person of the Eternal Word. That Divine Person terminates our act of worship, which consequently, from His Divinity, takes its character of Divine.

Hence it is that the devotion to the Sacred Heart is one of the greatest bulwarks of the doctrine of the Incarnation—of the union of two distinct natures, the Divine and the human, and their subsistence in one Divine Person, in such wise as that that Divine Person can say: 'This is My Body, This is My Blood;' *Vulnerasti Cor Meum*,—'Thou hast wounded My Heart;' 'They shall look on Him whom they have pierced;' or otherwise,—so as that we speak with accuracy and truth when we speak of the Body of God, of the Blood of God, of the Wounds of God, of the Heart of God.

In order rightly, fully, and clearly to apprehend, appreciate, and realise this, let us consider the history of the Sacred Heart in detail,—in Its formation,—in Its estate of death,—in Its estate of glory; and again,—in Its estate of abasement.

And first, as to Its formation.

That Sacred Heart once was not; and at a certain, given, ascertainable moment of time, It began to be. From all eternity It was not a reality, but a possibility,—and a contingent possibility, for Its existence depended on the concurrence of two wills; and neither of those wills lay under any necessity. Both were free. One was Divine; the other was human. The one was the Will of the Triune God; the other was the will of Mary. Unless those two wills had concurred, the

Sacred Heart of Jesus would not have existed. God had willed and decreed Its existence; but the accomplishment of that decree rested with her. She might have refused. God, it is true, had given her such a grace as He foreknew she would infallibly consent to; and yet this foreknowledge on His part in no way caused a single shadow of constraint to lie on the untrammelled freedom of her will. Her *Fiat* was the utterance of a free consent. The Creator longed to enter into His own creation, and to clothe Himself in the garments of the creature; but He would not enter, save with the consent of that creation, expressed by the lips of that creation's Queen.

Mary spoke the word. She uttered her *Fiat*; and on the instant there was accomplished a fourfold operation. The Third Divine Person, God the Holy Ghost, the Hypostatic Will, the Personal Love of the Father and the Son, descended and overshadowed the queenliest of His creatures, and there was formed within her, of her blood, a perfect human body, enshrining a human heart, which contained within it human blood. Secondly, in the selfsame instant there was, by the joint action, by the one creative energy of the Three Divine Persons, called out of nothingness into existence a perfect human soul, with a human intelligence and a human will. This was a direct creative act, and in this act the creature had no share. There was no coöperation of the Angels and none of **Mary**, save only that the formation of that human **body,** a formation dependent on, and effected by the concurrence of her will, was the moral cause, inducing God to the creation of that human soul. Thirdly, **in** the selfsame instant this human soul was infused into that human body, and the result of their union was the existence of a human life. Fourthly and finally, in the selfsame instant, that human body, with all it included and contained, animated by that human soul, was assumed at once and for ever into the unity of a Divine Person.

Now observe, this fourfold operation was the result of one instant. Had it taken two, the Heart that throbbed so close to the Immaculate Heart of Mary would not have been that Sacred Heart, which she in that instant worshipped, which she worships now, and which we, her subjects and her children, worship in union with her. Had that fourfold operation taken two instants instead of one for its accomplishment, that human heart would have subsisted in a human personality, and could not without idolatry have been worshipped, save with a higher degree of the same worship which Gabriel gave to Mary herself. It would only have been the holiest of creatures, and capable of only the highest created worship. But that Sacred Heart never subsisted, save in the unity of a Divine Person. There never was aught in Mary, distinct from her own personality, that was not Divine; and so never for an instant was Mary mother without being also Mother of God. No! the dignity of highest of creatures was reserved for Mary. She was left in her place as Creation's Queen, and as such she rendered to the Sacred Heart, derived from her own veins, and dependent for its existence on her own free will, the highest worship the creature could bestow on its Divine Creator. There was no sound to break the stillness of the night in the lonely chamber of that lowly cottage, but that lonely chamber was earth's holiest sanctuary, for it contained within it for the first time the Sacred Heart of Jesus, and Mary, Its first, and chiefest, and only worthy worshipper.

Again, we find the devotion to the Sacred Heart a bulwark of the faith,— of the doctrines of the Trinity, and of Creation, of the operations of the Holy Ghost, of the freedom of the human will, of the real maternity of Mary, and, consequently, of the real humanity of her Divine Son.

But now, let us change the scene. Let us go

from the House of Nazareth to the Hill of Calvary, from the midnight darkness of the Annunciation to the noonday darkness of the eclipse on the first Good Friday. Again we are in the society of Mary, and again in presence of the Sacred Heart. But the circumstances are changed. Mary is no longer the girl of fifteen summers, the joyful mother of the fairest among the sons of men. She has seen nearly fifty years pass by, and those years have been years of sorrow, and her sorrows have culminated in her desolation. She is a widow and childless. Her Son is dead. Before her eyes she sees, standing out against the sky, in the twilight of the eclipse, a ghastly Cross. On it hangs a crucified human body. The form and features are those of her only and well-beloved Son. But it is not her Son. A son is a man, and THAT is not a man. A man has soul and body, and that crucified body is animated by no living soul. The eyes are glazed, the limbs are motionless. It cannot return her embrace, It cannot look on her with the love of the old days of Nazareth. Mary is bereaved of her Son. No creature, no saint, no seraph can fathom the depths of her desolation. And yet she has one consolation. She is deprived indeed of her Son, but she is not deprived of the Sacred Heart. Before It she bends in lowliest adoration, to It she offers supremest worship. Death has severed the Soul of God from the Body of God. The lance of the Roman centurion has penetrated the inmost recesses of the Sacred Heart, and emptied It of the last drop of the Precious Blood of which It was the central source ; but death was powerless to separate Body or Soul or Heart or Blood from that Divine Person in Whom they one and all subsisted. The bereaved Virgin Mother adores the Sacred Heart of her Divine Son, and therein seeks and finds that consolation which no sympathy from any other human heart could avail to bestow.

At Nazareth we found her coöperating in the formation of the Sacred Humanity ; here we find her coöperating in Its destruction. Standing beneath the Cross, her eyes fixed on the Divine Victim, her will united with His will, she freely consented to the shedding of that Precious Blood, which by her free consent had been drawn from her own veins. She recognised the necessity of an infinite expiation for infinite sins — sins infinite because committed against an Infinite God. She knew our need, and His power to supply that need ; and so for us men and for our salvation she united her will with His, and freely and willingly offered her Divine Son to the Eternal Father.

It was a necessity, in order to the salvation of

the world, that the Sacred Heart should be bloodless, as well as that the Body of God should be
soulless. Every act of the Incarnate Word was of
an infinite value, and any act of His would have
been sufficient and superabundant for the redemption of ten thousand worlds, and that even had
every one of those worlds been ten thousand times
more wicked than the world which He came to redeem ; and yet it is also true that if He had not
been supernaturally strengthened in the Garden
of Gethsemani, and that if He had died there
before His time, the world would not have been
redeemed. He had not only offered His death for
the life of the world, but He had offered to the
Eternal Father a bloody death, and that offer had
been accepted. And so without shedding of blood
there could be no remission of sin.

Read in this light, the words of our text apply
to Mary with a fuller significance and a deeper
meaning than to any other through whom or for
whom He died. She looked on Him whom she had
pierced, and hence it is that to her the Church
applies the Scripture : *Vulnerasti Cor Meum, amica Mea, sponsa Mea,*—'Thou hast wounded My
Heart, My sister, My spouse.' Not only had Mary
her share, and the chief share, in the wounding of
the Sacred Heart, in virtue of her coöperation with

the Great High-Priest in His immolation of Himself as the Victim of Expiation; but in virtue also of her redemption, which made that immolation necessary, He was her Redeemer as well as Mary Magdalen's and ours. 'My spirit' (she sings in her Magnificat) 'hath rejoiced in God my Saviour.' Apart from that Bloodshedding, Mary would not have had the grace of her Immaculate Conception or the dignity of her maternity. Nay! in one sense Mary cost Him most of all. It cost Him more to redeem Mary than to redeem any other or all of the human race—for Mary's was the noblest of redemptions. Others He redeemed from original sin at least, if not also from actual sin, but Mary He redeemed in such wise as that no shadow of the original transgression, and no stain of sin should rest for an instant on her soul. 'Thou art all fair, O My love, and there is no spot in thee.' Her Immaculate Conception, says one of the most loving of the children of Mary, was the first white blossom that bloomed on the ruddy stem of His blood-stained Cross.

Here again you see how the devotion to the Sacred Heart is a bulwark of doctrine, guarding the mysteries of the Redemption of mankind, in its universality and completeness, and of the Immaculate Conception of Mary.

And now, once more, let us change the scene. Let us go from without the walls of the earthly Jerusalem, to within the walls of the Jerusalem that is above. Again we find ourselves in the society of Mary, and again in presence of the Sacred Heart. It is the selfsame Heart, but no longer bloodless and silent, without a human soul. He had power to lay down His life, and He had power to take it again. In His hands were the issues of life and death. He triumphed over hell and the grave, and He has ascended into heaven, leading captivity captive. He is exalted far above principalities and powers, and He is set down clothed in the garment of His Humanity at the right hand of the Eternal Father. That human Heart is beating with the pulses of a human life within that human Body which is seated on the great White Throne; and Mary, whom we saw at Nazareth as the Mother of Joy, and again at Calvary as the Mother of Sorrow, we see now as the Mother of Glory. She is crowned a Queen on the Holy Mountain of the Heavenly Zion, she is seated on the highest of created thrones, and from that throne she pays a royal homage to the Sacred Heart. Her worship now is the same in kind and in degree with her worship then. It is infinite and supreme. It can suffer no increase and no decrease. Its

K

character may and does differ, but its essence remains the same.

Again do we find the devotion to the Sacred Heart a bulwark of the faith, guarding the doctrines of the Resurrection, the Ascension, and the Session at the right hand of the Eternal Father.

Such is the vision of faith—the Sacred Heart in heaven adored by its first and chiefest worshipper. We are on earth, in the house of our bondage, in the land of our exile; we turn our eyes to the everlasting hills; we seek solace in our sorrows by rising on the wings of faith and fleeing in spirit to the land that is very far off. Our worship and our love strive to pierce the clouds, and unite with the worship and the love of the heart of Mary.

And yet with all this, there is an unsatisfied craving in the human heart—the heart that loves longs for the *presence* of the object loved. This craving also God has satisfied. The worship of the Sacred Heart is no worship of a thing of the past, which we recall by an effort of the memory, and gaze at through the vista of eighteen centuries. It is a reality of the present, existing in our midst and on our altars. We fix our gaze on the sacramental veils that shroud It from our eyes of flesh, and the eye of faith can discern It beneath them, and

we know and can say, It is here, and not there.
We know that within the roundness and the white-
ness of the consecrated Host there lives the Ever-
living Jesus—ever living with a twofold life—the
Divine **Life** of His Divine Person and the human
life of His human Soul. Wrapt in the Sacramental
Species lies His human Body, which enshrines His
Sacred **Heart**, the **Living Chalice** of the Precious
Blood, the Blood drawn from the veins of Mary,
shed in His Passion, and reassumed in His Resurrection. This is the object of our faith when the
sound of the bell breaks on our ears at the eleva-
tion in the Mass; and again when we see Him
raised on high at holy Benediction. And this object of our faith is the object also on which our
love centres, for we 'look on Him Whom we have
pierced.'

We have a vested interest in that Sacred Heart.
It has special relations to us, and we to it. It was
pierced and emptied of Its contents for the human
race, and to that human race we, by virtue of our
humanity, belong. But that is not all. It has a
personal, individual, separate relation to each one
of us; and each one of us has a personal, individual,
separate relation to It. The Good Shepherd laid
down His life for His sheep—He knows, He says,
His sheep, and calleth them by name; and so not

merely for us as possible, or as undistinguishable parts of one vast whole, as units of the human race; but for each one of us separately, for every individual member of the flock of God, He offered Himself and laid down His Life as a sacrifice, and shed His Blood as a ransom. We were each individually present and known to the human Soul of Jesus as It agonised in the garden and on the Cross; and for each individual soul He offered His whole sacrifice, as if that one had been the only soul that needed to be redeemed; as if He had offered Himself and been accepted, and come and suffered and died for that single soul.

Hence the tremendous, overwhelming agony of the Crucified. It was not a mere agony of body, it was an agony of soul as well; and an agony, moreover, not to be measured by the ordinary limits of a three hours' agony, but to be multiplied as many times as there were men to redeem, and again as many times as, in His foreknowledge, He foresaw that there should be mortal sins to expiate.

Thus then we have two distinct relations to the Sacred Heart; and in both relations we have been crucifiers of our Divine Lord. In the first place, simply as human beings sprung from Adam, and therefore conceived in iniquity, and born dead in trespasses and sins, we cost that Sacred Heart a pang which our non-existence would have spared It. Had we never existed, there would have been one soul fewer to redeem from original sin, and the load of His sufferings would have been, by so much less.

But that is only one of the sufferings which we individually have cost Him. St. Paul tells us, that by every mortal sin we have crucified the Son of God afresh, and put Him to an open shame. Our contrition for each separate mortal sin, as well as its absolution, was purchased and merited separately by another and another intensity of agony of soul.

What a terrible thought is that of our share in the Crucifixion! Our souls sink within us and our hearts fail as we realise it—as we look on Him Whom we have pierced. It is truly a terrible thought to the sinner as yet unconfessed and unabsolved; but to the sinner who has confessed and turned away from his sins, His words are indeed, ' *Vulnerasti Cor Meum*,' but they are also ' *Amica Mea, sponsa Mea*.' That sinner, but a few minutes ago foul with sin, the enemy of God, is now His friend and His spouse. Not only are his sins remembered no more against him, but he is become indeed and in truth an object of the Divine friendship and the **Divine love.** Nay, more, the very fact of his **sins in the past gives** him a special claim— a title to the love of Jesus in the present, a love in proportion to the very number and enormity of his sins.

Does not a mother lavish the richest treasures of her love on the **child who has** cost her most? Is not the depth and strength and tenderness of her love in the present in proportion to the bitterness of her anguish in the past? And so is it with the long-suffering of Him Whose love passeth the love of women. The Good Shepherd has a greater tenderness and a deeper love for the lost sheep that has strayed from the fold, and wandered in the wilderness, and been torn by the briers, and mangled by the wild beasts, than for the ninety-and-nine, for the just who need no repentance. They are His own words—'I came not to call the just, but sinners to repentance.' He was called 'the Friend of sinners.' His chief friend on earth was the woman who had been 'a sinner.' He admitted her to the society of the virginal Disciple and of His Immaculate Mother on the hill-top of Calvary ; and that to make manifest the two classes of human beings who had cost Him most, and therefore whom He loves the most—the innocent and the penitent ; the woman that was a sinner, the woman that was sinless. Mary Magdalene cost Him much, but Mary Immaculate cost Him more.

How can we then give way to doubt or despair in presence of the Sacred Heart. We know, indeed, that there is a 'measure of iniquity'—that there is a certain number of sins allotted to each human being, which its Maker will pardon, to cancel and annul which the Precious Blood was offered and accepted and shed, and beyond which God will not go. We do not know how many are allotted to each one of us individually, or how far we have already gone, or how near we have come to the fatal termination. But this we do know, that at that termination no one of us here present has yet arrived. The term of our life is the period of our probation. The only reason why sinners are permitted to live on is the yet present possibility of their conversions— is because they have not yet filled up the measure of their iniquity—they have not yet committed their last sin. When they have committed that, in that moment they die.

Here, then, is matter for fear and trembling, but in no way for despair. On the contrary, hope and gratitude are the two affections which such a thought naturally begets in the soul; and these two issue in a twofold act, an act of sorrow for the past, and an act of firm purpose and efficacious resolve for the future to go and sin no more. Those are the dispositions requisite for a good confession. Thereby all our sins, however many, and whatever their malignity, are cancelled. We are once more in the state of grace. This is an effect of the mystical application of the contents of the Sacred Heart which takes place in the Sacrament of Penance; and it prepares us for, and entitles us to, the real and true, substantial and physical application of the Precious Blood to our souls, which takes place in Holy Communion. We have a capacity and a right to do more than adore—to receive the Sacred Heart within ourselves. There the Heart that was wounded on the Cross is placed in closest proximity to our own; and the Blood that was shed for us—to redeem us, is shed also within us—to sanctify us. The Bloodshedding on the Cross was —that we might live, and not die. The Bloodshedding within us is—that we should not only have life, but should have it more abundantly.

The Sacred Heart in Heaven is the well-spring and the central source of the Precious Blood. It is contained within It; but It is not confined within It. Were it so, that Sacred Heart would be straitened, and the love of that Heart would be limited. It demands an overflow, and through the channel of the Sacrament of Love, which testifies and satisfies the love of the Incarnate God, the Blood of God is poured forth from the Heart of God, and flows from Its spring in the Heavenly Jerusalem, even to the uttermost ends of the earth. It is the Well of Living Water whose streams make glad the City of our God.

Moreover, a day will come when the Sacred Heart will beat with one vibration throughout the entire Body. The will of God will be done by the sons of earth as by the angels of heaven. Man was made at the first a little lower than them, but then he shall be exalted far above them, and that by reason of his consubstantiality with the God-man, the Incarnate Word—by reason of his incorporation into the Mystical Body—by reason of his consanguinity with the Son of Mary through the Sacred Heart.

Those blessed spirits who for ages have worshipped their Maker in the beauty of holiness, and have added to His accidental glory by the perfection of their unwearying, unceasing service, will in their unselfish humility do honour to the Mystical Body of their human Sovereign, as It ascends with Him into the Eternal Home. It is His Immaculate Bride who cometh up from the desert leaning upon the Arm of her Beloved; and they will

admire the Queen in her beauty. They have been
her servants and her ministers as she wended her
way through the wilderness of the world; recog-
nising her even when defiled with the dust and
mire of the journey, with the sweat and stains of
the conflict and the race; but now that the race is
run and the warfare over, and the day of labour
has seen its close, and Purgatory is in the past,
and she is a glorious Church, not having spot or
wrinkle or any such thing, they rejoice in, as they
marvel at, her beauty, for she is beautiful with the
beauty of God, shining with the glory of the Father, and stamped with the image of His Christ.

What Mary is individually, that the Church
of God is collectively—the Daughter of God, the
Spouse of God, nay also, in a manner, the Mother
of God! A shadow of the Divine maternity lies
also upon her. There has been an overshadowing
by the Holy Ghost of her also. 'Christ,' says the
Apostle, 'has been formed in you.' And again, 'Ye
bear God in your bodies.' Such is the perfection
of our union with the Divine life. As God's children, 'now are we the sons of God; and it doth
not yet appear what we shall be.' As God's chosen
spouse and bride, our life is hid with Christ in
God. Of Him and of His mystic bride the words
are true in a deeper, fuller, and more real sense

than of the first Adam and his spouse. They two shall be one flesh. In virtue of that shadow of the Divine maternity, we add our share to the one great living whole — the heavenly Divine life of the Mystical Body, when the last enemy is laid low, and death is swallowed up in victory.

Naturally the Body of God exists in heaven, glorified, exalted in majesty, worshipped by angels, seated on the great White Throne beyond the stars, and with Mary by Its side; and that Body contains the Sacred Heart, and that Heart is the Living Chalice of the Precious Blood.

But supernaturally the selfsame Body of God exists on earth, beneath the same roof, within the same four walls as ourselves, within a few feet of us, inside the Tabernacle: glorified—yes; but in the garments of humility, wrapped in the swaddling clothes of the Sacred Species: worshipped by angels—yes; but fitfully, and feebly worshipped by His own, by the sons of men. Within that Body is the Sacred Heart, and within that Heart is the Precious Blood, the Blood that once was Mary's, the Blood of the Everlasting Covenant, the Blood of Gethsemani and Calvary, the Blood of the Scourged and Crucified God.

Thus does He, Who covered the nakedness of His crucified Body with His own Blood as with a vesture of royal purple, cover the nakedness of our souls, and invest them with the likeness of His Royalty.

'Who is this,' said the prophet, 'who cometh from Edom, with dyed garments from Bozrah, glorious in His apparel?'

'And who are these?' said the Angels of God in the hearing of the rapt Evangelist, the virginal Disciple whom Jesus loved, the Apostle who leaned against and listened to the beatings of the Sacred Heart, the old Man of Patmos, whose eyes were bleared with the weary watchings of his rocky exile, but whose spiritual vision brightened, and became clearer and more clear as the days of his earthly pilgrimage approached their end, and the day of his dissolution was at hand. 'Who are these in white robes, and whence come they?' 'They are those who have come out of great tribulation, and have washed their robes, and made them white in the Blood of the Lamb.'

Not only was the great multitude that no man can number, gathered out of every kindred and nation and people and tongue, redeemed by the Precious Blood; but the common participation of that Blood is the principle of its unity and of its life. God has made of one Blood, the Blood of the Crucified, all the kindreds of the earth. The

Sacred Heart in its world-wide overflow knows no frontiers, no nationalities, no diversities of race, or clime, or language. It is pervasive as the light of the sun, or as the air which that light illuminates. In the One Body, there is no earth-born distinction of Jew and Gentile, of male and female, of bond and free. All are one, through the Precious Blood, and the point of unity is the Sacred Heart from which It flows.

The final, perfect, complete, and adequate triumph of the Sacred Heart will be at the latter day, when not only the natural Body of the Crucified, but the Mystical Body also will be no longer on earth but in heaven. There, just as the heart of man naturally is the central source of that blood in which is the life, which all the members of the body share, and by which they are one and all quickened and invigorated, whereby they one and all have life and health, and strength and beauty; so also will the Sacred Heart of the Son of Man be the central source of life and health and strength and beauty to all that vast body of men who are one in Him, that vast race of human beings who, by partaking of His Sacred Humanity, have been made partakers of the Divine Nature with which it is inseparably united, who have thereby become of one heart and mind and will, of one sentiment and understanding and knowledge and purpose and desire.

There will be a perfect individuality, preserved untouched to each; there will be no confusion of individualities, no merging of them in God. They will not be consumed or lost in that supernatural, heavenly, divine Unity, any more than the Sacred Humanity is consumed in the furnace of the Divinity with which it is united, or any more than the separate operation of the human will of the God-Man is lost in the operation of the Divine will with which it is in closest, undeviating, and indissoluble concord. There will be as many real separate hearts and minds and wills as there are individual men; but each will be subdued and brought under to the obedience of Christ. The spiritual beauty, the supernatural glory wherewith the Bridegroom adorns His chosen Bride, is not something extrinsic or merely external. It is not merely an outer garment to cover her nakedness, and to hide her deformity and her defilement. Were the garment of Divine grace merely an external imputation of the justice of Christ, as Calvin in his ignorance and his unbelief imagined, there might indeed be an external beauty, but it would be but the beauty of a whited sepulchre, fair to the eye, but within full of rottenness and dead men's bones. True, the Queen has her garment of gold, wrought about with divers colours; yet she, the King's Daughter, is all glorious WITHIN. As grace has its residence in the central soul, so also has its correlative, that glory which takes its place, or which rather is its issue and efflorescence. That glory will shine out at the latter day through the immortal, incorruptible bodies of the risen. As the light communicates its brightness to the lantern in which it is enclosed, so will the light of the Beatific Glory radiate from the souls of the blessed, and glorify also the risen bodies which enshrine them. There shall be no need of the sun or of the moon in the Heavenly City, for the glory of God shall lighten it, and the Lamb shall be the light thereof.

Such is the devotion to the Sacred Heart of Jesus in its dogmatic aspect. It is a mighty bulwark of the faith. It is simply impossible for a man to have an intelligent devotion to the Sacred Heart, and to have wrong ideas as to the Christian doctrine. But its dogmatic is not its only value. It has also its devotional value. Not only is it richly indulgenced by the Vicar of Jesus Christ, but most special promises have been made by Christ Himself to all who practise it. He revealed to that humble nun whom He chose as His instrument for its propagation, the Blessed Margaret Mary, that to all who are devout to His Sacred Heart He will give all the graces necessary for their state of life; that He will give peace in their families, and prosperity to their undertakings, and consolation in their difficulties; that sinners shall find in His Heart a fountain and boundless ocean of mercy; that tepid souls shall become fervent, and fervent souls more fervent; that He will be their secure refuge in life, and especially at the hour of death. Nay, that if they even but expose and honour a picture of the Sacred Heart in their houses, those houses shall be especially blessed.

Whether, then, we regard it in its dogmatic or in its devotional aspect, there is no devotion more adapted to meet the needs of the age in which we live than the devotion to the Sacred Heart of Jesus. It is a continual protest against the Sadducean spirit of the day. It is an antidote to the vapid, dreamy mysticism and pietistic sentimentalism, to the materialism and sensual naturalism, as well as to the proud, rebellious intellectualism which pervades and poisons the air we breathe. It is a grand masculine devotion, preëminently the devotion of strong natures; it fortifies the soul, and lays deep, solidly, and firmly in the reason and the will, the foundations of the spiritual life. Regard then, study and practise this devotion; you will find it a centre round which your other devotions will gather, a foundation whence they will derive steadiness and solidity, and a living light diffusing to them its own brightness and vitality.

VII.

Joseph virum Mariæ.

Joseph the husband of Mary. *St. Matt.* i. 16.

St. Gregory Nazianzen, whose body lies beneath the roof of St. Peter's, whose soul has been with God for more than a thousand years, and whose writings have illuminated the Church of Christ, when speaking the praises of the dead husband of his sister Gorgonia, says :—' Will you that I describe him in one word? He was *her* husband. And what need I more say?' So also we, speaking of the glorious St. Joseph, virtually say all that can be said when we repeat the words of the Evangelist :—*Joseph virum Mariæ*—' Joseph the husband of Mary.'

There are two truths which it is very necessary that we should have clearly in our minds, and keep steadily before us, throughout the whole course of what we say in his honour.

And the first is, that Jesus Christ had no earthly father. He had a real, true, earthly, human mother; but His only Father was Divine, the

Eternal and Unbegotten, the First Person of the ever-blessed Trinity. He derived His Humanity from the veins of Mary, from the fountains of her blood, from the most precious matter to be found in entire creation, and that in a miraculous and supernatural manner through the operation of the Holy Ghost. 'The Holy Ghost shall come upon thee, and the power of the Most High shall overshadow thee, and therefore also the Holy which shall be born of thee shall be called the Son of God.'

The second truth which with equal clearness we must have in view is, that although Jesus did not derive His Humanity from the substance of Joseph, and although Joseph and Mary had severally bound themselves to God by a vow of perpetual virginity, which they ever faithfully observed, yet apart from this, and in every other way, Joseph was really, truly, and properly the husband of Mary. It was a valid, lawful, real, true, and proper matrimonial bond, which joined together in one those two virginal human beings.

It is mutual consent which effects matrimony. By such mutual matrimonial consent, the one spouse delivers and makes over to the other that dominion over himself or herself which has hitherto been his or her own. Such consent, once expressed,

is in every case irrevocable. In this case it was
dictated by no private judgment, nor was it the
issue of any merely human affection. It was the
result of a Divine inspiration. In giving this matrimonial consent, Mary and Joseph were fulfilling
an eternal decree, and accomplishing the Divine
will. Once given, it could not be retracted.
What God had joined together man could not
set asunder.

St. Augustine says that three things are required and suffice to the essence of matrimony:

1. *Fidelity.* And what fidelity between earthly
spouses was ever like that of Joseph and Mary,
who were in all things and ever of one judgment, of one heart and will, of one sentiment and
affection?

2. *Sacramentality.* And what earthly union
of human beings ever so visibly shadowed forth,
so perfectly symbolised, so vividly and adequately
represented, the union of the Divinity and the
Humanity, in the one person of the Incarnate
Word; the union between Him, the Heavenly
Bridegroom, and the Catholic Church, His immaculate Bride; and the union which He estab-
lishes between Himself and the regenerate and
sanctified human soul?

3. *Offspring.* And what offspring of two earthly

parents was ever like Him who was at once Son of Man, begotten of the substance of Mary, and Son of God, consubstantial with the Eternal Father?

Theirs was, then, a true and real matrimony. It was not a fictitious matrimony—a make-believe, a mere blind, under cover of which the Incarnation was to take place. Mary was not a single but a married woman. She was as really a married woman as she was really a virgin. In that only was Joseph not her husband, as to which the coöperation of Joseph was not necessary.

But although Jesus did not derive the substance of His human Body from the veins of Joseph, yet there lay on Joseph, as it were, a shadow of the Divine paternity. Among his contemporaries, Joseph had the name and reputation of father of Jesus. Jesus was, 'as was thought, the son of Joseph.' Men said, ' His father and mother we know.' 'Is He not the son of the carpenter? Is He not the son of Joseph?'

But this common reputation was the least of His dignities. Not only from those who were ignorant of the divinity of Jesus, of His miraculous conception, and of the perpetual virginity of Joseph and Mary, had Joseph this honour; he had it from the pen of the Evangelist, and from the lips of Mary herself. The Evangelist writes of him : ‘When IIis *parents* brought in the child Jesus ;’ and again, ‘His *father* and mother marvelled at those things which were said of Him.’ And Mary’s own words, when after the three-days’ loss she found her divine Child seated before the doctors in the Temple at Jerusalem, were : ‘Son, Thy *father* and I have sought Thee sorrowing.’ Those words, moreover, we must remember, were not merely the words of even the Evangelist or of Mary ; they were words written by the one and uttered by the other ; but they were also in both cases dictated by the Holy Ghost, by Whom both were inspired. The name of Father of Jesus was thus bestowed on Joseph, not by man, but by God Himself.

But, farther, along with this name, Joseph possessed the reality which that name represents. He possessed a real parental authority over the Divine Child ; to which there corresponded, on IIis part, a real filial subjection.

Jesus, dying on the Cross of Calvary, commended John to Mary with, ‘Woman, behold thy son !’ He manifested thereby a singular love to the virginal disciple by an act which was at once a communication to him of a name proper to Himself, and a substitution of him in His own place of filial solicitude for IIis own Mother. But ‘Father

of Jesus' is a greater name than 'Son of Mary.'
The name of 'father' is a name of authority, and
the dignity of Jesus exceeds infinitely the dignity
of Mary.

The fourth dignity of St. Joseph consisted in
this, that he was in a manner superior to, and
head of both Mary and Jesus. 'The head of the
woman is the man,' says St. Paul; and St. Peter
writes in his Epistle, 'Wives, be subject to your
husbands, as Sarah obeyed Abraham, calling him
lord.' So Mary reverenced her husband as her
head and lord. He was in reality the head of that
holy household. As such, it was to him, and not
to Mary, that God revealed His will, that he
should take the young Child and His Mother and
go into the land of Egypt; and again, that he
should return thence with them into his own city.
To him also, and not to Mary, God gave the commandment, 'Thou shalt call His name Jesus.'
And when, after the finding in the Temple, Jesus,
the boy of twelve years old, went down with His
parents to Nazareth, it is written that 'He was
subject unto *them*'—subject to Joseph as well as
to Mary; to Mary as in reality His Mother, and
so possessing a real parental authority over Him;
to Joseph as really her husband, and so really
sharing with her that authority.

When **God** gives a special name, He at the same time constitutes a man in the position, condition, and **office** which that name expresses. **A** name **divinely** given is not a mere **empty name.** It is a sign and pledge of that which it conveys. Joseph possessed and exercised a real parental authority over **the Incarnate Word; and He** returned him a filial submission, subjection, obedience, and reverence. Those **were his due,** and that in two ways :—

In the first place, inasmuch as Joseph had **communicated** to him from the **First Person** of the **Blessed Trinity,** from Whom all paternity in heaven and earth is named, a shadow of the parental authority which is appropriated or specially attributed to Him as He is the **Eternal Father.**

And secondly, inasmuch as he, in his character of husband **of Mary, and in** virtue of that community of goods which exists **between** the spouses, as a result of the matrimonial bond, **and** whereby the goods **of** the one belong to **the other also,** had his share in whatsoever she possessed. **Married** persons together form one civil person, and the property of each is possessed in common, and belongs **to** both. Joseph therefore had his share, as Mary's husband, in Mary's greatest treasure, the prerogative of her parental authority. **Again, as a treasure**

hid in a field belongs to the owner of that field, so
Jesus, Who was conceived in Mary, belonged to
Joseph.

These four dignities and prerogatives of Joseph I have stated and described, not in words
taken from the rapturous outpourings of some
ecstatic saint, however lawful and laudable it would
have been to do so, but in the cold, measured,
rigorous language of the Schools, and following
Suarez as my guide; and this advisedly, in order
that we may see how solid are the foundations on
which devotion to St. Joseph rests. I might have
spoken of the opinion of various holy writers that
he was sanctified in the womb, like Jeremias and
the Baptist; that he was preserved by a special
grace of God throughout his life from the com-
mission of any, even venial, sin; that he had an
infused foreknowledge of the Passion, and a mystical antecedent compassion therewith; and that
his holy virgin body has been assumed into heaven,
along with his glorified soul; but for the reason
given, I have preferred to confine myself to these
four dignities, as four fountains from which we
may derive a conception of his sanctity in its kind
and in its degree.

In conceiving and estimating the sanctity of a
Saint, we may proceed in either of two ways—

either by way of comparison or by way of contemplation. Now, in order to comparison, there must be some points of agreement and resemblance between those whom we compare. But to whom shall we liken St. Joseph—*Quis inventus est similis illi?* And so with whom shall we compare him? He differed from all others, whether angels or men, in his office. It was his own peculiar prerogative, and therefore his sanctity, whether as the preparation, disposition, accompaniment, result, or crown of his office, is in a category of its own. Let us, then, consider St. Joseph by way of contemplation, and particularly in his relation to ourselves. To him the Church applies the words of the Psalm: *Constituit eum dominum domus Suæ, et principem omnis possessionis Suæ*—'He made him master of His house, and ruler of all His possession.' God, as God, is the Lord, because God, as God, is Creator and Preserver in their existence, of all His creatures. But this title of *Lord*, along with a real lordship and dominion which it denotes, has been bestowed on and belongs to the Man Jesus Christ, as He is the Incarnate Word. He has a possession alike by right of primogeniture and by right of conquest,—as the First-born of every creature, and again, as having conquered death and hell, and risen triumphant and victorious from the grave, the First-fruits from the earth, and the First-begotten from the dead. The Man Jesus Christ has, then, a possession, and that possession is a House, built up of living stones on a foundation laid by Himself, after His own idea and plan, and resting on Himself as its *Lapis Angularis*, its chief corner-stone. Moreover, this House is a temple— the Temple of God, and that Temple is twofold.

'Destroy this Temple, and in three days I will raise it up,' said Jesus to the Jews. But He spake of the temple of His Body. His Body, created, finite, human, passible, and mortal, was the Temple of God in the highest possible sense; for in it dwelt 'the fulness of the Godhead corporally;' and from that human Soul which inhabited It was constantly ascending heavenwards an adequate, because an infinite, worship of Its Maker. The Infinite God was infinitely worshipped by the Man Jesus Christ, by reason of the Infinity of the Divine Person, Who was Incarnate, Whose that Humanity was, and Who offered that worship. It was absolutely impossible that the Creator God should receive a higher worship than that of the created human Soul of the Son of Mary;—and the Body which enshrined that Soul, and from which that worship streamed forth, was therefore, in the highest possible sense, the Temple of God.

But again, we read in Holy Scripture of another **Body** of Christ, of a mystical **Body**—an extension of that natural Body, and of which that natural Body is the head, and men in union therewith are the members.

This Body also is a **Temple** from which a worship is constantly ascending towards **God**. It therefore is also, in a special sense, the House of God, and in a special manner His possession. 'Ye,' says St. Paul to the Corinthians, 'are the Body of Christ, and members of member;' and to the Colossians, 'He is Head of the Body the Church.' Singly, individually, and apart, we are each of us members of Christ and temples of the Holy Ghost. Unitedly, collectively, and as a whole, we form a Body, with Him as our one Head in heaven. As a body and a soul meet in the unity of a human person, and form one whole man, and as the human and divine natures met in the unity of a Divine Person, and formed — *Totum Christum*—one whole Christ; so do the members of the mystical Body, the Catholic Church, and their Divine Head meet in the unity of one moral person, and form one individual whole—the Mystical Christ.

Farther, from the essential unity of the members with their Head, and so one with another, springs that community of goods, and that identification of interests, which is the solid foundation of the intercourse and commerce between earth and heaven—the practical as well as the speculative communion of Saints.

Hence it is, 1. That our feeble prayers and imperfect works have power and value before God, because they lie before Him, not in their own inherent nakedness and poverty, but as assumed into the unity of, and identified with the human intercessions and works of the Incarnate Word.

2. Hence also it is that the prayers and works of one individual man may produce an effect, not only in himself, but on another member of the mystical Body, for whose benefit they are applied. We can pray and satisfy, not only for ourselves, but also for others, our brethren of the One Family, our fellow members of the One Body, our fellow worshippers within the One Temple.

This intercession, moreover, is ordained and regulated according to the mind and will of God, Who has 'constituted angels and men in a wonderful order'—alike in heaven and on earth. His creatures lie before God, not as a multitude of separate, dissevered, dissociated, unconnected, independent units, but as a body or society, composed of members between each of whom is an intimate, essential union, interdependence, and association. Just as in the natural order we depend on others in all the relations of life, so in the supernatural order God wills us to depend on others, our fellow creatures, in all the relations of the supernatural life.

We depend on others, and others depend on us. Our own salvation may, in the Divine plan, depend on a prayer being offered, or on an act of satisfaction being done on our behalf by another member of the mystical Body; and again, the salvation of another may, according to the same Divine scheme, depend upon a prayer being offered, or an act of satisfaction being done by us on his behalf. Looked at from the natural point of view, and with the eye of sense, these things appear to be mere coincidences—the result of circumstances and chance. Looked at from the supernatural point of view, and with the eye of faith, they are seen to be links in a hidden chain of supernatural second causes, and to be integral parts of the Divine plan.

Even of men while yet on earth, weighed down by their corruptible bodies, and struggling with sin, this is true. Their prayers are powerful with God, not for themselves only, but also for others. Much more, then, is it not true in regard of those

who are freed **from** the burden of their mortal
bodies, and who, **as the case** may be, are either
already clothed with incorruptible, impassible, immortal, and glorious bodies, as in the case of Mary;
or who, as **is** the case with the generality of the
Saints, are existing in Heaven, in the enjoyment
of the Beatific Vision, but as yet with the imperfection of disembodied spirits, and in expectation of the final consummation — to wit, the
resurrection of the body. If the effectual fervent
prayer of a just man, who, although just, may
yet, as says the Scripture, fall seven times, availeth
much; of how much more avail must be the intercession of those spirits of just men made perfect,
who stand in the immediate presence of the unveiled God?

The doctrine, which is of Divine faith, that the
beatified members of the Church triumphant in
Heaven continually intercede for the members of
the Church militant on earth, that they may be
victors in their struggle with the world, the flesh,
and the devil, is a natural consequence and result
of the doctrine of the perfect unity of the mystical
Body; as is also that other doctrine, that satisfactions made by them while yet on earth, and so in
the estate of meriting, and which have not been
required for the satisfaction of their own offences,

may be applied on behalf of others, their brethren and fellow members, by those to whom that power has been committed and belongs.

This mutual interest, interchange, and inter-dependence of all the members of the whole mystical Body one with another, is what we mean when we say, 'I believe in the Communion of Saints.'

But, farther, the interference, intervention, and mediation of the Saints in our affairs is directly under the Divine regulation and ordination. It follows a certain order, and proceeds on certain principles. We on earth have relations with the Blessed in Heaven, not only collectively, but individually. There are particular Saints with whom our relations are more direct and more intimate than with others, and those are what are called our protectors or patrons. Their interest in us, and our correlative duties towards them, are alike founded in a real relation existing between us and them. This relation may be very diverse; but the diversity in no case affects its reality. Certain Saints are patrons of countries, of religious orders, of various classes, conditions, and callings, or of individuals. This relation may be a similarity between their past condition while on earth, and the present condition and circumstances, or sympathies or sufferings, of their clients. Or, again, they may have been placed, either by others or by an act of their own will, under the patronage and protection of a special Saint, as, for instance, of him whose name they bear. In any case, the relation is a real one, resting on a solid ground, and the effect of a true cause. And the result of this relation is the interest of that Saint in, and the efforts of that Saint for, those with whom he is specially and personally connected. This Communion of Saints is no mere poetical fancy; it is not a beautiful dream, the growth of a luxuriant imagination; it is no devout exaggeration: it is a simple fact and an objective power.

Now, the Incarnate Word condescended, not only to assume our human nature, but also to enter into special relations with individual human persons,—to have disciples, to have friends, and to have parents. This last was the most intimate of all His human relations. Not only did He depend for the existence of His Body on Mary's free gift from her own substance, and for His daily bread, on the solicitude and toil of Joseph; but He also entered into a relation of subjection to both: *Subditus erat illis*—'He was subject to them'—to His 'parents,' to their parental authority. And this was a real relation. It was not a shadow, much less an affectation of a relation; and it was

M

not interfered with by the fact that they were His creatures, and that He was their Creator; any more than the royalty of a king interferes with his filial relation and filial subjection to the parental authority of the queen-mother, although she is in reality his subject.

Our Divine Lord, then, willed to depend on Joseph as His protector for the care of His Body, and for the supply of its daily wants. When that office of protection was no longer necessary, Joseph passed away, an old man and full of years, to his rest in the bosom of Abraham. Jesus and Mary could not follow him thither; they could not transfer their habitation, and reconstitute the Holy Family of Nazareth in the Limbus of the Fathers. They had work to do on earth. But when that work was done, and the Body of the dead Christ found rest in the sleep of death, His Soul went to seek Joseph, to glorify him with the Beatific Vision, to deliver him from his place of temporary exile, to bring him again from his second Egypt of Expectation, and to appoint him another work;—or rather to set him again in his old office, but in a new relation.

During the great Forty Days, the soul of Joseph was with the risen Jesus. This is certain, for we know that He who, as an ancient father says, descended alone into Limbus, returned thence with a great multitude. He brought thence with Him all those whose purgation was at an end, and by whose sufferings the Divine Justice had been satisfied; or in the words of Holy Scripture, He returned, 'leading captivity captive.' Among those immaculate souls was certainly St. Joseph's, and as certainly his beatified soul did not enter Heaven before the Ascension of Jesus, to Whom it belonged to open the gate of Heaven to all believers, and to enter as the first-fruits from the earth, and as the first-begotten from the dead. The soul of Joseph, then, was in the company of the risen Jesus, hearing and seeing, so to speak, if we may use such words of a disembodied spirit, those things which He said and did after His Resurrection; and that, not as an uninterested listener and spectator, but attentive as one who had a place and a part, a position and an office in the work of the risen Christ for the application of the one Sacrifice once offered upon the Cross of Calvary. That work was the organisation of the mystical Body, the constitution and construction of that supernatural society which was to extend to every land and throughout all time, which was to be the depositary of the promises, the channel of Divine grace, and the custodier, witness, and in-

terpreter of Divine truth to the children of men.
And when at last the work of the great Forty
Days was ended, Joseph ascended with his Son to
Heaven, and received there a place, and his own
place in the celestial hierarchy, an office, and his
own office in the economy of God's dealings with
mankind. We have now to define what that pre-
cise place was, and wherein that office consisted.

There was now—at the date of the Ascension
—alike in Heaven and on earth, a Body of Christ.
In Heaven was His human, natural, but glorified
Body, exalted to the Throne of God, and seated at
the right hand of the Eternal Father. On earth
was a mystical Body, still struggling wearily on
the way of its pilgrimage. Escaped it was indeed
from the land of Egypt, delivered from the house
of bondage, passed through the Red Sea ; but beset by enemies on every side, far from home, a
pilgrim in the desert, a stranger in a strange land,
looking forward to and tending towards the place
of its rest beyond the Jordan, in the Land of Promise, in the Heavenly Jerusalem, the City of
Peace. To care for this Body, to watch over and
protect it with a father's love, to be its created
providence, was the destiny and function of Joseph
in Heaven. His Divine Son made him Lord of
His House and Ruler of all His Possession.

Such is the line of thought suggested by the Decree of the Vicar of Jesus Christ, whereby, listening to the prayers of the whole Episcopate, and so of the whole body of the faithful throughout the world, he has solemnly declared St. Joseph Patron of the Catholic Church, and placed himself and all his subjects anew under his august and powerful protection. He compares him with his type the first Joseph, the son of the Patriarch Jacob, who, for the welfare of his people, became ruler over all the land of Egypt. He speaks of his sublime dignity, as next to that of his Immaculate Spouse. He reminds us that the Church has always specially sought his intercession in times of trouble. And finally he indicates the fittingness of the present time—when the Church is beset by enemies on every side, and so weighed down by heavy calamities, that ungodly men imagine that the gates of hell have at length prevailed against her—for a renewed and solemn act of consecration of the whole Church on earth to St. Joseph, in his relation as Patron and Protector of the mystical Body of Jesus Christ. What, then, is our relation to St. Joseph, and how is it affected by this Decree, directed to the whole world, and so individually to each one of us?

In the first place, it intensifies our vision of

the Holy Family, of the Created Earthly Trinity, once on earth and now in Heaven. Secondly, it deepens our sense of dependence on God and God's creatures whom He has so highly exalted. And finally, it increases our confidence in St. Joseph as a power with God, actively operating on our behalf.

First, it intensifies our vision of the Holy Family. St. Joseph stands no longer in the background in our conception of that Family. He is set forward in his relation as Head of the Holy House—as when the angel was wont, in the days of Nazareth and Egypt, to confer with him in that capacity. He appears to us no longer, as in an old painting of the Nativity, standing in the background, and almost less noticeable than the shepherds and the magi; but rather, as in a picture of the Flight into Egypt, where he leads the way of the wilderness. Here the Virgin Mother and the Divine Child are still the principal figures; but St. Joseph has an active post, guiding, planning, solicitously careful, and casting his mantle for protection round the Body of Jesus Christ.

A spiritual writer observes, that while Mary was in a manner associated by our Divine Lord with Himself in His priestly office, inasmuch as she ministered directly by an act of her will, and

by her spoken words, in effecting the existence of
His Human Body, and ministered also in their
joint oblation of that Body on the Altar of the
Cross; St. Joseph seems rather to resemble a
deacon to whose office it pertains not to consecrate,
but to bear the Sacred Body, to care for Its safety
and the fitness of Its surroundings. In another
way too St. Joseph resembles a deacon; it is in his
function of solicitude for the temporalities of the
Church. To fulfil this was the proximate occa-
sion of the ordination of the first deacons by the
Apostles. And it seems to be more with the outer
than with the inner life of the Church that, in his
relation of Protector and Patron, St. Joseph is
immediately concerned, although with the inner
life he has also much to do. He is, for instance,
the special patron of the *Bona Mors.* To him we
instinctively turn to procure for us the final grace
of a good death. Still it is with ecclesiastical
politics and diplomacy and finance, with the external constitution and regulation of the Church,
with her defence against the assaults of the powers
of this world, with the reparation of the ravages of
heresy and schism, with the temporal power and
civil princedom and the other prerogatives and
privileges of the Vicar of Jesus Christ, that St.
Joseph has very specially to do. To this the

Decree seems to point; and it is noteworthy that, looking back into the history of the past, the dark days of trouble and calamity appear to have been those during which the faithful were, by a Divine instinct, drawn to have especial recourse to the intercession of St. Joseph.

Secondly, these thoughts deepen our sense of dependence, not only upon God, but upon God's creatures; and tend to make us realise the hierarchical character of the Divine Dispensation. There is One Mediator of God and men, the Man Jesus Christ; but the mediation of the Saints in no way derogates from the oneness of His Mediation—nay, it is its legitimate natural result and necessary consequence. Those only fail to apprehend this who are outside the unity of the One Mystical Body. And yet even they, were they to consider the ways of God within their own souls, and His marvellous association of themselves with Him in the work of their salvation, might obtain some light as to the beauty and fitness of this other association of His creatures with Himself in the affairs of men. Our own conversion to God must be an act of our own intellect and will, in order that it may be a real human act, and our own act, as well as the act of God. He acts, in the processes of our spiritual life, not only in us, but with us.

We work out our salvation, and He works in us to will and to do according to His own good pleasure. God does not simply *use* us. He makes us fellow workers together with Him; we really coöperate with Him. We are God's coadjutors in the work of our own salvation. And as with us, so also with His Saints in Light. God gives to the prayers of the Saints, to those acts of their intellects and wills, a value and efficacy and power with Himself, in virtue of and corresponding to their sanctity, and by reason of their identification with Jesus Christ, His Son and their Lord.

But if this be so with the saints in general, with how much more force does it not apply to St. Joseph? Grave writers teach that he obtains his requests *non impetrando sed imperando*—not so much by prayer as by command. What mean those singular words? Certainly not that Joseph has power to coerce the will of Jesus Christ, so as that He should grant a favour contrary to the dictates of His own reason. But as certainly they do not mean nothing. The words would be meaningless if they did not indicate a real distinction between the prayers of the parents of Jesus and those of other Saints. They mean this:—In the treasure-house of Divine graces there are certain which God wills to bestow at the intercession and through the intervention of special Saints, and not otherwise.   Else why should we invoke one Saint rather than another? and why should we invoke the lesser as well as, and sometimes rather than, the greater Saints ? God, then, wills to bestow certain graces and benefits at the intercession of and through St. Joseph, which no lesser and no other Saint can procure.   Moreover, nothing that he asks can be but entirely agreeable to the Human Will of the Son of Mary ; and asking in his character of foster-father, and as clothed with his parental authority, nothing that he asks will he ask in vain.   As in the house of Nazareth the fact that all the commands of Joseph were entirely agreeable to Him whom he commanded, and were in no way opposed to the dictates of either His Divine or His Human Will—as this in no way interfered with or affected the reality of his parental authority, and the correlative filial subjection of the Son of Mary—so also now as to the intercessions of Joseph, which are said to be rather by way of command than of prayer, their supreme accordance with the will of the glorified Jesus in no way deprives them of their character of command.

How powerful and efficacious are the intercessions of St. Joseph we learn from St. Theresa, who tells us that many and great graces, nay, all that she had, she had got from God through the intercession of St. Joseph.

It is most important for us clearly to apprehend, and adequately to realise, this distinction between the intercessions of Joseph and Mary and those of other Saints; as, failing to do this, we should not only deprive ourselves of a glorious truth, which sheds a vivid light on the Divine condescensions and the exaltation of the creature, but there would also be lacking to us a most powerful motive of confidence in our recourse to St. Joseph. It is true, as we have said, that as in a picture of the Holy Family, Jesus and Mary have the principal place, and first attract the eye, while Joseph stands in the background, so has it been in the devotional life of the Church of God. And yet, just as in that picture, Joseph, although in the background, is still there—for without him the picture would be incomplete—so also in the Church of God, and in the minds of Christian men, St. Joseph has always had his place as an object of devotion, although not in the explicit, pronounced, and developed form in which he is presented to us to-day. Devotion to him is not a luxuriant outgrowth of Christianity; it is an integral part, essential and necessary to its completeness.

There may have been two reasons for the fact

that hitherto the devotion to St. Joseph has not been such as it must in future of necessity become. First, because in the early ages of the Church, when she had to teach the first principles of Christianity to Jew and Gentile, to barbarian and idolater, to men of carnal, sensual, and earthly minds, there might have been danger in proposing in all its fulness the parental character of Joseph, lest men should fail to grasp the truth that from Joseph Jesus did not derive His Sacred Humanity. Secondly, we may discern a reason in the fact of Joseph's being the created earthly shadow of the Eternal Father. The First Divine Person, Whom in the Earthly Trinity he represents, has ever indeed His place in men's minds, but He is not so prominent and consciously present to our thoughts as the Son and the Holy Ghost. We turn naturally and instinctively to Jesus, Who, in virtue of His Humanity, is one with us, flesh of our flesh and blood of our blood; and next to the Holy Ghost, as sent to us, and shed abroad in our hearts; and last of all our thoughts ascend to the Unseen and the Unsent, the First Person, the Eternal Father. So also it is with the Incarnate Word, with the Spouse of the Holy Ghost, and with him on whom lay the shadow of the Divine Paternity.

These are reasons which suggest themselves.

Whether they be *the* reasons we know not—it is the secret of God.

But now the time has come, and the words of Solomon are verified: 'He that is the keeper of his Master shall be glorified.'

How can we better commend ourselves to Jesus and to Mary than by our devotion to Joseph? To whom can we commit the care of our temporal affairs better than to him who cared for those of Mary and Jesus?

Whom better can we invoke to watch over our dying beds than he, the pillow of whose dying bed was smoothed by the hands of Mary, and who breathed his last in the arms of Jesus?

Finally, St. Paul teaches us that if one member suffer, all the members suffer with it. And how much more must not the sufferings of the head redound to and affect the members of the body! Our divinely-constituted Head is at this moment suffering. He is in captivity; his free intercourse with the members of the mystical Body throughout the world is grievously interfered with, if not practically interrupted. The action of the Church is thus in a manner paralysed. Now it is in our power, powerless as we are in the natural order individually to hasten the time of his deliverance, and the triumph of the Church of God; and the means which God has put in our power is prayer, and a principal means is prayer to St. Joseph.

Remember that on Easter-Day the voice of the Vicar of Christ was not heard in the Piazza of St. Peter's, and that this year the *Benedictio Dei Omnipotentis* has not descended on the world. Let that thought sink deep down into your souls; and may it bear its fruit in at least our daily prayer to him whom the Incarnate Word has made Master of His House and Ruler of all His Possession!

THE END.

London : Robson & Sons, Printers, Pancras Road.

A Select Catalogue of Books

PUBLISHED BY

BURNS, OATES, & CO.,

17 & 18, PORTMAN STREET,

AND

63, PATERNOSTER ROW.

BOOKS LATELY PUBLISHED

BY MESSRS.

BURNS, OATES, & CO.,

17 & 18, Portman Street, and 63, Paternoster Row.

Memorials of those who Suffered for the Faith in Ireland in the Sixteenth, Seventeenth, and Eighteenth Centuries. Collected from Authentic and Original Documents by MYLES O'REILLY, B.A., LL.D. 8vo, 7s. 6d.

"A very valuable compendium of the martyrology of Ireland during the three, or rather two, centuries of active Protestant persecution. The language of many of these original records, written often by a friend or relative of the martyr, is inexpressibly touching, often quite heroic in its tone."—*Dublin Review.*

"Very interesting memories."—*Month.*

Life of St. Thomas of Canterbury. By Mrs. HOPE, Author of "The Early Martyrs" Cloth extra, 4s. 6d.

A valuable addition to the collection of historical books for Catholic readers. It contains a large collection of interesting facts, gleaned with great industry from the various existing Lives of St. Thomas, and other documents.

"Compiled with great care from the best authors."—*Month*.

"The rich covers of this splendidly-bound volume do not, as is often the case, envelop matter unworthy of its fair exterior. This is a volume which will be found useful as a present, whether in the college or school, for either sex."—*Weekly Register*.

"An agreeable and useful volume."—*Nation*.

"A more complete collection of incidents and anecdotes, combined with events of greater weight, could not be compressed into so compact, yet perfectly roomy, a space."—*Tablet*.

By the same Author.

Life of St. Philip Neri. New Edition. 2s. 6d. ; cheap edition, 2s.

NARRATIVE OF MISSIONS.

The Corean Martyrs. By Canon SHORT-LAND. Cloth, 2s.

A narrative of Missions and Martyrdoms too little known in this country.

"This is a notice of the martyrs who have fallen in this most interesting mission, and of the history of its rise and progress up to the present day."—*Tablet*.

"No one can read this interesting volume without the most genuine admiration of, and sympathy with, such zeal and constancy."—*Literary Churchman*.

MISSIONARY BIOGRAPHY.

1. *Life of Henry Dorie, Martyr.* Translated by Lady HERBERT. 1s. 6d. ; cloth, 2s.

"The circulation of such lives as this of Henry Dorie will do much to promote a spirit of zeal, and to move hearts hitherto stagnant because they have not been stirred to the generous deeds which characterise Catholic virtues."—*Tablet.*

2. *Théophane Vénard, Martyr in Tonquin.* Edited by the Same.   2s. ; cloth elegant, 3s.

" The life of this martyr is not so much a biography as a series of letters translated by Lady Herbert, in which the life of Théophane Vénard unfolds itself by degrees, and in the most natural and interesting way.   His disposition was affectionate, and formed for ardent friendship ; hence, his correspondence is full of warmth and tenderness, and his love of his sister in particular is exemplary and striking.   During ten years he laboured under Mgr. Retord, in the western district of Tonquin, and his efforts for the conversion of souls were crowned with singular success.   During the episcopate of his Bishop no less than 40,000 souls were added to the flock of Christ, and Vénard was peculiarly instrumental in gathering in this harvest."—*Northern Press.*

" We cannot take leave of this little volume without an acknowledgment to Lady Herbert for the excellent English dress in which she has presented it to the British public ; certainly, no lives are more calculated to inspire vocation to the noble work of the apostolic life than those of Dorie and Vénard."—*Tablet.*

3. *Life of Bishop Brute.*   Edited by the Same.

The Martyrdom of St. Cecilia : a Drama. By ALBANY J. CHRISTIE, S.J.   With a Frontispiece after Molitor.   Elegant cloth, 5s.

" Well-known and beautiful drama."—*Tablet.*
" The receipt of the fourth edition of this beautiful play assures us that our own opinion of its merits has been shared by a wide circle of the Catholic public.   The binding is exquisite, and the picture of St. Cecilia is a work of art."—*Weekly Register*

The Life of M. Olier, Founder of the Seminary of St. Sulpice; with Notices of his most Eminent Contemporaries. By EDWARD HEALY THOMPSON, M.A. Cloth, 4s.

This Biography has received the special approbation of the Abbé Faillon, Author of " La Vie de M. Olier;" and of the Very Reverend Paul Dubreul, D.D., Superior of the Seminary of St. Sulpice, Baltimore, U.S.

Edited by the Same.

The Life of St. Charles Borromeo. Cloth, 3s. 6d.

Also, lately published, by Mr. THOMPSON.

The Hidden Life of Jesus: a Lesson and Model to Christians. Translated from the French of BOUDON. Cloth, 3s.

" This profound and valuable work has been very carefully and ably translated by Mr. Thompson. We shall be glad to receive more of that gentleman's publications, for good translation, whether from the French or any other language, is not too common amongst us. The publication is got up with the taste always displayed by the firm of Burns, Oates, and Co."—*Register.*

" The more we have of such works as ' The Hidden Life of Jesus,' the better."—*Westminster Gazette.*

" A book of searching power."—*Church Review.*

" We have often regretted that this writer's works are not better known."—*Universe.*

" We earnestly recommend its study and practice to all readers." —*Tablet.*

" We have to thank Mr. Thompson for this translation of a valuable work which has long been popular in France."—*Dublin Review.*

" A good translation."—*Month.*

BURNS, OATES, & CO., 63, *PATERNOSTER ROW, E.C.*

Devotion to the Nine Choirs of Holy Angels,
and especially to the Angel Guardians. Translated from the Same.   3s.

"We congratulate Mr. Thompson on the way in which he has accomplished his task, and we earnestly hope that an increased devotion to the Holy Angels may be the reward of his labour of love."—*Tablet.*

"A beautiful translation."—*The Month.*

"The translation is extremely well done."—*Weekly Register.*

Library of Religious Biography. Edited by EDWARD HEALY THOMPSON.

Vol. 1. THE LIFE OF ST. ALOYSIUS GONZAGA, S.J.   5s.

"We gladly hail the first instalment of Mr. Healy Thompson's Library of Religious Biography. The life before us brings out strongly a characteristic of the Saint which is, perhaps, little appreciated by many who have been attracted to him chiefly by the purity and early holiness which have made him the chosen patron of the young. This characteristic is his intense energy of will, which reminds us of another Saint, of a very different vocation and destiny, whom he is said to have resembled also in personal appearance—the great St. Charles Borromeo."—*Dublin Review.*

"The book before us contains numberless traces of a thoughtful and tender devotion to the Saint. It shows a loving penetration into his spirit, and an appreciation of the secret motives of his action, which can only be the result of a deeply affectionate study of his life and character."—*Month.*

Vol. 2. THE LIFE OF MARIE EUSTELLE HARPAIN ; or, the Angel of the Eucharist.   5s.

"The life of Marie Eustelle Harpain possesses a special value and interest apart from its extraordinary natural and supernatural beauty, from the fact that to her example and to the effect of her writings is attributed in great measure the wonderful revival of devotion to the Blessed Sacrament in France, and consequently throughout Western Christendom."—*Dublin Review.*

"A more complete instance of that life of purity and close union with God in the world of which we have just been speaking is to be found in the history of Marie Eustelle Harpain, the sempstress of Saint-Pallais. The writer of the present volume has had the advantage of very copious materials in the French works on which his own work is founded, and Mr. Thompson has discharged his office as editor with his usual diligence and accuracy."—*The Month.*

Vol. 3. THE LIFE OF ST. STANISLAS KOSTKA. 5s.

"We strongly recommend this biography to our readers, earnestly hoping that the writer's object may thereby be attained in an increase of affectionate veneration for one of whom Urban VIII. exclaimed that, although 'a little youth,' he was indeed 'a great saint.'"—*Tablet.*

"There has been no adequate biography of St. Stanislas. In rectifying this want, Mr. Thompson has earned a title to the gratitude of English-speaking Catholics. The engaging Saint of Poland will now be better known among us, and we need not fear that, better known, he will not be better loved."—*Weekly Register.*

The Life of S. Teresa, written by herself: a new Translation from the last Spanish Edition. To which is added for the first time in English THE RELATIONS, or the Manifestations of her Spiritual State which the Saint submitted to her Confessors. Translated by DAVID LEWIS. In a handsome volume, 8vo, cloth, 10s. 6d.

"The work is incomparable; and Mr. Lewis's rare faithfulness and felicity as a translator are known so well, that no word of ours can be necessary to make the volume eagerly looked for."—*Dublin Review.*

"We have in this grand book perhaps the most copious spiritual autobiography of a Saint, and of a highly-favoured Saint, that exists."—*Month.*

The Life of Margaret Mary Alacoque. By the Rev. F. TICKELL, S.J. 8vo, cloth, 7s. 6d.

"It is long since we have had such a pleasure as the reading of Father Tickell's book has afforded us. No incident of her holy life from birth to death seems **to be** wanting, **and** the volume appropriately closes with an account of her beatification."—*Weekly Register.*

"It is one of those high-class spiritual biographies which will **be** best **appreciated in** religious communities." — *Westminster Gazette.*

"Of **Father** Tickell's labours we **can say with pleasure that he** has given us a real biography, in which the Saint is everything, and the biographer keeps in the background."—*Dublin Review.*

"We can only hope that the life may **carry on, as it is worthy** of doing, the apostolate begun **in our country by one who** our Lord desires should be 'as a brother to **His servant,** sharing equally **in** these spiritual goods, united with **her to His own** Heart for ever.'"—*Tablet.*

"The work could hardly **have been done in a** more unpretending, and **at the same** time more **satisfactory, manner** than in the volume now **before us."**—*Month.*

The Day Hours of the Church.   Latin and English.   Cloth, 1s.

Also, separately,

THE OFFICES **OF PRIME AND COMPLINE.**   8d.

THE OFFICES **OF** TIERCE, **SEXT, AND NONE.**   3d.

"Prime **and** Compline are the morning and evening **prayers** which the Church has drawn up for her children; and, **for our part,** we **can wish for nothing better.** We **know not where** an improvement could be suggested, and therefore we see not why anything should **have** been substituted for them. . . . **Why** should not their **use be** restored? Why should **they not become the standard devotions of all** Catholics, whether **alone or in their** families? Why may **we not** hope to have **them more solemnly** performed—chanted even every day in **all religious** communities; or, where **there is a** sufficient **number of persons, even in** family chapels?"—*Cardinal Wiseman.*

"These beautiful little books, which **have received the im**primatur of **his Grace the** Archbishop, are a zealous **priest's** answers to the most **eminent** Cardinal's questions—such **answers as** would have gladdened his heart could they have been given **when** first demanded. **But the Cardinal lives in his** successors

BURNS, OATES, & CO., 17, PORTMAN STREET, W.

and what he so greatly desired should be done is in progress of full performance."—*Tablet*.

"The publication of these Offices is another proof of what we have before alluded to, viz., the increased liturgical taste of the present day."—*Catholic Opinion*

POPULAR DEVOTION.
Now ready.

Devotions for the Ecclesiastical Seasons,
consisting of Psalms, Hymns, Prayers, &c., suited for Evening Services, and arranged for Singing. Cloth, 1s. Also in separate Nos. at 2d. each, for distribution, as follows :—

1. Advent and Christmas.
2. Septuagesima to Easter.
3. Paschal Time.
4. Whitsuntide.
5. Sundays after Pentecost.
6. Feasts of our Lady.
7. Saints' Days.

Music for the whole, 1s. 6d.

"A valuable addition to our stock of popular devotions."—*Dublin Review*.

Church Music and Church Choirs: 1. The Music to be Sung; 2. The proper Singers; 3. The Place for the Choir. 2s.

"The special value of this pamphlet, and the seasonableness of its circulation, lie in this: that it attempts to solve—and, we believe, does really solve—several important points as to the proper kinds of music to be used in our public Offices, and more especially at High Mass."—*Tablet*.

"We earnestly recommend all who can do so to procure and study this pamphlet."—*Weekly Register*.

"Masterly and exhaustive articles."—*Catholic Opinion*.

Liturgical **Directions for** *Organists,* **Singers,** and **Composers.** Contains the Instructions of the Holy See on the proper kind of Music for the Church, from the Council of Trent to the present time; and thus furnishes choirs with a guide for selection. Fcp. 8vo, 6d.

New Meditations *for each Day in the Year* on the Life of our Lord Jesus Christ. By a Father of the Society of Jesus. With the imprimatur of his Grace the Archbishop of Westminster. Second Edition. Vols. I. and II., price 4s. 6d. each; or complete in two vols., 9s.

"We can heartily recommend this book for its style and substance; it bears with it several strong recommendations. . . . It is solid and practical without being dreary or commonplace." *Westminster* **Gazette.**

"A work of great practical utility, and we give it our earnest recommendation."—*Weekly Register.*

The Day Sanctified : being **Meditations and** Spiritual Readings for Daily Use. Selected from the Works of Saints and approved writers of the Catholic Church. Fcp., cloth, 3s. 6d.; red edges, 4s.

"Of the many volumes of meditation on sacred subjects which have appeared in the last few years, none has seemed to us so well adapted to its object as the one before us."—*Tablet.*

"Deserves to be specially mentioned."—*Month.*

"Admirable in every sense."—*Church Times.*

"Many of the Meditations are of great beauty. . . . They form, in fact, excellent little sermons, and we have no doubt will be largely used as such."—*Literary Churchman.*

Our Father: Popular Discourses on the Lord's Prayer. By Dr. EMANUEL VEITH, Preacher in Ordinary in the Cathedral of Vienna. (Dr. V. is one of the most eminent preachers on the Continent.) Cloth, 3s. 6d.

"We can heartily recommend these as accurate, devotional, and practical."—*Westminster Gazette.*

"We are happy to receive and look over once more this beautiful work on the Lord's Prayer—most profitable reading."—*Weekly Register.*

"Most excellent manual."—*Church Review.*

Little Book of the Love of God. By Count STOLBERG. With Life of the Author. Cloth, 2s.

"An admirable little treatise, perfectly adapted to our language and modes of thought."—*Bishop of Birmingham.*

NEW BOOK FOR HOLY COMMUNION.

Reflections and Prayers for Holy Communion. Translated from the French. Uniform with "Imitation of the Sacred Heart." With Preface by Archbishop MANNING. Fcp. 8vo, cloth, 4s. 6d.; bound, red edges, 5s.; calf, 8s.; morocco, 9s.

"The Archbishop has marked his approval of the work by writing a preface for it, and describes it as 'a valuable addition to our books of devotion.' We may mention that it contains 'two very beautiful methods of hearing Mass,' to use the words of the Archbishop in the Preface."—*Register.*

"A book rich with the choicest and most profound Catholic devotions."—*Church Review.*

BURNS, OATES, & CO., 63, PATERNOSTER ROW, E.C.

Holy Confidence. **By Father ROGACCI, of the**
Society of Jesus.   One vol. 18mo, cloth, 2s.

"**As an attack on the** great **enemy,** despair, **no work could be**
more effective ; while **it** adds another to a stock of books **of devo-**
tion which is likely **to be** much prized."—*Weekly Register*.

"This little book, addressed **to** those 'who strive to **draw**
nearer **to God and to** unite themselves more **closely** with Him,'
is one of the most **useful** and comforting that we **have** read for a
long time.   We earnestly **commend** this little **book** to all
troubled souls, feeling **sure** that they will **find in it** abundant
cause for joy and consolation."—*Tablet*.

* * *

The Invitation Heeded: **Reasons for a**
Return **to Catholic Unity.   By** JAMES KENT
STONE, **late President of Kenyon College, Gambier,**
Ohio, and of Hobart College.   Cloth, 5s. 6d.

"A very important contribution to our polemical literature,
which **can hardly fail to be a standard work on the Anglican con-**
troversy."—*Dr. Brownson in the New York Tablet.*

. Of this able work **3000 have already been sold in America.**

* * *

The New Testament Narrative, **in the**
Words **of the Sacred Writers.   With Notes,**
Chronological Tables, and Maps.   A book for
those who, as a matter of education or of devotion,
wish to be thoroughly well acquainted with the
Life of our Lord.   What is narrated by each of
His Evangelists is woven into a continuous and
chronological narrative.   Thus the study of the
Gospels is complete and yet easy.   Cloth, 2s.

"The compilers **deserve great praise for the manner in which**
they have performed **their task.   We commend this little volume**
as well and **carefully printed, and as furnishing its readers, more-**

over, with a great amount of useful information in the tables inserted at the end."—*Month.*

"It is at once clear, complete, and beautiful."—*Catholic Opinion.*

Balmez: Protestantism and Catholicism compared in their Effects upon European Civilisation. Cloth, 7s. 6d.

*** A new edition of this far-famed Treatise.

The See of St. Peter. By T. W. ALLIES. A new and improved edition, with Preface on the present State of the Controversy. 4s. 6d.

Lallemant's Doctrine of the Spiritual Life. Edited by Dr. FABER. New Edition. Cloth, 4s. 6d.

"This excellent work has a twofold value, being both a biography and a volume of meditations. Father Lallemant's life does not abound with events, but its interest lies chiefly in the fact that his world and his warfare were within. His 'Spiritual Doctrine' contains an elaborate analysis of the wants, dangers, trials, and aspirations of the inner man, and supplies to the thoughtful and devout reader the most valuable instructions for the attainment of heavenly wisdom, grace, and strength."—*Catholic Times.*

"A treatise of the very highest value."—*Month.*

"The treatise is preceded by a short account of the writer's life, and has had the wonderful advantage of being edited by the late Father Faber."—*Weekly Register.*

"One of the very best of Messrs. Burns and Co.'s publications is this new edition of F. Lallemant's 'Spiritual Doctrine.'"—*Westminster Gazette.*

The Rivers of Damascus and Jordan: a Causerie. By a Tertiary of the Order of St. Dominick. 4s.

"Good solid reading."—*Month.*

"Well done, and in a truly charitable spirit."—*Catholic Opinion.*

"It treats the subject in so novel and forcible a light, that we are fascinated in spite of ourselves, and irresistibly led on to follow its arguments and rejoice at its conclusions."—*Tablet.*

Eudoxia: a Tale of the Fifth Century. From the German of IDA, COUNTESS HAHN-HAHN. Cloth elegant, 4s.

"This charming tale may be classed among such instructive as well as entertaining works as 'Fabiola' and 'Callista.' It adds another laurel to the brow of the fair Countess."—*Weekly Register.*

"Instructive and interesting book."—*Northern Press.*

Tales for the Many. By CYRIL AUSTIN. In Five Numbers, at 2d. each; also, cloth, 1s.; gilt edges, 1s. 6d.

"Calculated to do good in our lending-libraries."—*Tablet.*

"We wish the volume all the success it deserves, and shall always welcome with pleasure any effort from the same quarter." —*Weekly Register.*

"One of the most delightful books which Messrs. Burns and Oates have brought out to charm children at this festive season." —*Catholic Opinion.*

In the Snow; or, Tales of Mount St. Bernard. By the Rev Dr. ANDERDON. Cloth neat, 3s. 6d.

"A collection of pretty stories."—*Star.*

"An excellent book for a present."—*Universe.*

BURNS, OATES, & CO., 17, *PORTMAN STREET, W.*

" A capital book of stories."—*Catholic Opinion.*

" An agreeable book."—*Church Review.*

" An admirable fireside companion."—*Nation.*

" **A very** interesting **volume** of tales."—*Freeman.*

" **Several successive stories are related by** different people assembled together, **and thus a greater scope is** given for variety, not only of **the matter, but also the** tone of each story, according to the temper **and position of the** narrators. Beautifully printed, tastefully **bound, and reflects great credit on the** publishers."

" **A** pleasing **contribution."**—*Month.*

" **A** charming **volume. We congratulate Catholic** parents and **children on the appearance of a book which may** be given by the **former with advantage, and read by the latter with pleasure and edification."**—*Dublin Review.*

By the same Author.

The Seven Ages of Clarewell : A History of a Spot of Ground. Cloth, 3s.

" We **have an attractive work from the pen of an author who** knows how **to combine a pleasing and lively style with the** promotion **of the highest principles and the loftiest aims. The** volume before **us is beautifully bound, in a similar way** to ' In the Snow,' by **the same author, and is therefore very** suitable for a present."—*Westminster Gazette.*

" A **pleasing novelty in the style and character of** the book, which is **well and clearly sustained** in the manner it is carried out."—*Northern Press.*

" Each stage furnishes the material for a dramatic scene; are very well hit off, and the whole makes up a graphic picture."—*Month.*

" ' Clarewell ' will give not only an hour of pleasant reading, but will, from the nature of the subject, be eminently suggestive of deep and important truths."—*Tablet.*

WORKS BY LADY GEORGIANA FULLERTON.

Life of Mary Fitzgerald, a Child of the Sacred Heart. Price 1s.; cloth extra, 2s.

BURNS, OATES, & CO., 63, PATERNOSTER ROW, E.C.

Rose Leblanc.   A Tale of great interest.
Cloth, 3s.

Grantley Manor.   (The well-known and favourite Novel).   Cloth, 3s. ; cheap edition,
2s. 6d.

Life of St. Frances of Rome.   Neat cloth,
2s. 6d. ; cheap edition, 1s. 8d.

Edited by the Same.

Our Lady's Little Books.   Neat cloth, 2s. ;
separate Numbers, 4d. each.

Life of the Honourable E. Dormer, late of
the 60th Rifles.   1s. ; cloth extra, 2s.

Helpers of the Holy Souls.   6d.

Tales from the Diary of a Sister of Mercy.
By C. M. BRAME.

CONTENTS : The Double Marriage—The Cross and
the Crown—The Novice—The Fatal Accident—The
Priest's Death—The Gambler's Wife—The Apostate
—The Besetting Sin.

Beautifully bound in bevelled cloth, 3s. 6d.

" Written in a chaste, simple, and touching style."—*Tablet.*
" This book is a casket ; and those who open it will find the
gem within."—*Register.*
" Calculated to promote the spread of virtue, and to check that
of vice ; and cannot fail to have a good effect upon all—young
and old—into whose hands it may fall."—*Nation.*
" A neat volume, composed of agreeable and instructive tales.

BURNS, OATES, & CO., 17, *PORTMAN STREET, W.*

Each of its tales **concludes with a** moral, which supplies food for reflection."—*Westminster* **Gazette.**

" They are well and **cleverly told, and** the volume **is neatly got up."**—*Month.*

"Very well told ; all full of religious allusions and expressions."—*Star.*

" Very well written, and life-like—many very pathetic."—*Catholic Opinion.*

" An excellent **work ; reminds us** forcibly of Father Price's ' Sick Calls.' "—*Universe.*

" A very interesting series of tales."—*Sun.*

By the Same.

Angels' Visits : A Series of Tales. With
Frontispiece and Vignette. 3s. 6d.

" The tone of the book is excellent, and it will certainly make itself a great favourite with the young."—*Month.*

" Beautiful collection of Angel Stories. All who may wish to give any dear children a book which speaks in tones suited to the sweet simplicity of their innocent young hearts about holy things cannot do better than send for ' Angels' Visits.' "—*Weekly Register.*

" One of the prettiest books for children we have seen."—*Tablet.*

" A book which excites more than ordinary praise. We have great satisfaction in recommending to parents and all who have the charge of childrenthis charming volume."—*Northern Press.*

" A good present for children. An improvement on the ' Diary of a Sister of Mercy.' "—*Universe.*

" Touchingly written, and evidently the emanation of a refined and pious mind."—*Church Times.*

" A charming little book, full of beautiful stories of the family of angels."—*Church Opinion.*

" A nicely-written volume."—*Bookseller.*

" Gracefully-written stories."—*Star.*

Just out, ornamental cloth, 5s.

Legends of Our Lady and the Saints: or, Our
Children's Book of Stories in Verse. Written

BURNS, OATES, & CO., 63, *PATERNOSTER ROW, E.C.*

for the Recitations of the Pupils of the Schools of
the Holy Child Jesus, St. Leonards-on-Sea.
Cheap Edition, 2s. 6d.

"It is a beautiful religious idea that is realised in the 'Legends
of Our Lady and the Saints.' We are bound to add that it has
been successfully carried out by the good nuns of St. Leonards.
The children of their Schools are unusually favoured in having so
much genius and taste exerted for their instruction and delight.
The book is very daintily decorated and bound, and forms a
charming present for pious children."—*Tablet.*

"The 'Legends' are so beautiful, that they ought to be read by
all lovers of poetry."—*Bookseller.*

"Graceful poems."—*Month.*

Edith Sydney: a Tale of the Catholic
Movement. By MISS OXENHAM.   5s.

"A novel for the novel-reader, and at the same time it is a
guide to the convert and a help to their instructors."—*Universe.*

"Miss Oxenham shows herself to be a fair writer of a contro-
versial tale, as well as a clever delineator of character."—*Tablet.*

"A charming romance. We introduce 'Edith Sydney' to
our readers, confident that she will be a safe and welcome visitor
in many a domestic circle, and will attain high favour with the
Catholic reading public."—*Nation.*

"Miss Oxenham seems to possess considerable powers for the
delineation of character and incident."—*Month.*

Not Yet: a Tale of the Present Time.
By Miss OXENHAM.   5s.

"The lighter order of Catholic literature receives a very welcome addition in this story, which is original and very striking.
The author is mistress of a style which is light and pleasant.
The work is one to which we can give our heartiest commenda-
tion."—*Cork Examiner.*

"We are indebted to Miss Oxenham for one of the most interesting sensational Catholic tales yet published."—*Catholic Opinion.*

"Wholesome and pleasant reading, evincing a refined and cultivated understanding."—*Union Review.*

"Miss Oxenham's work would rank well even among Mudie's novels, although its one-volume form is likely to be unfavourable in the eyes of ordinary novel-readers ; but, in nine cases out of ten, a novelette is more effective than a regular novel, and any more padding would have merely diluted the vivid and unflagging interest which the authoress of 'Not Yet' has imparted to her elegantly-bound volume. The plot is as original as a plot can be ; it is well laid and carefully and ably worked out."—*Westminster Gazette.*

Nellie Netterville : a Tale of Ireland in the Time of Cromwell. By CECILIA CADDELL, Author of " Wild Times." 5s. ; cheap edition, 3s. 6d.

" A very interesting story. The author's style is pleasing, picturesque, and good, and we recommend our readers to obtain the book for themselves."—*Church News.*

" A tale well told and of great interest."—*Catholic Opinion.*

" Pretty pathetic story—well told."—*Star.*

" Pretty book-history of cruelties inflicted by Protestant domination in the sister country—full of stirring and affecting passages."—*Church Review.*

" Tale is well told, and many of the incidents, especially the burning of the chapel with the priest and congregation by the Cromwellian soldiers, are intensely interesting."—*Universe.*

" By a writer well known, whose reputation will certainly not suffer by her new production."—*Month.*

Marie ; or, the Workwoman of Liège. By CECILIA CADDELL. Cloth, 3s. 6d.

" This is another of those valuable works like that of ' Marie Eustelle Harpain.' Time would fail us were we to enumerate either her marvellous **acts of charity, or** the heroic sufferings she endured for the sake of others, or **the** wonderful revelations with which her faith and charity were rewarded."—*Tablet.*

"The author **of** ' Wild Times,' and other favourite works, **is** to be congratulated **on** the issue **of a** volume which is of more service than any **book** of fiction, however stirring. It is **a beau-**tiful work—beautiful **in its** theme and in its execution."—*Weekly Register.*

" Miss Caddell has **given us** a very interesting biography of ' Marie Sellier, the **Workwoman** of Liège,' known in the 17th century as ' Sœur Marie Albert.' **Examples** such as that so grace-fully set forth in this volume **are** much **needed among us."—**
Month.

The Countess of Glosswood: a Tale of the Times of the Stuarts. From the French. 3s. 6d.

"The tale is **well written, and** the translation seems cleverly done."—*Month.*

"**This volume is prettily got up,** and **we can** strongly **recom-**mend it to **all as an excellent and instructive little** book **to place** in the hands **of the young."—***Westminster* **Gazette.**

"An excellent **translation, and a very** pretty tale, well told." —*Catholic* **Opinion.**

" This **is a pretty tale** of a Puritan conversion in **the time of** Charles **II.,** prettily **got up,** and a pleasing **addition to our** lending-libraries."—*Tablet.*

" This **tale** belongs to **a class** of which we **have had to** thank Messrs. Burns **for** many beautiful specimens. Such books, while they are delightful reading **to us who are** happily Catholics, have another important merit—they set forth the claims of Catholicism, and **must do a vast** deal **of good** among Protestants who casually meet with and peruse them. The book before us is beautifully got up, and would **be an ornament to any table."—***Weekly Register.*

BURNS, OATES, & CO., 17, *PORTMAN STREET, W.*